Fi
SPIDERS

An Identification Guide for Southern Africa

MARTIN R. FILMER
revised by NORMAN LARSEN

*To my son Robert, an inspiration to everyone
who meets him. And to my daughter Leigh, who
encouraged me to keep going for his sake.*

Acknowledgements

I would like to thank the following for their many contributions: Dr Ansie Dippenaar-Schoeman for her inspiration, spontaneous help and advice, and for always being there; the late Moya Hartmann, who triggered my interest in and love for spiders; Dr Alan Kemp, my mentor and friend in things natural; Des Louw, who provided the first conspectus which allowed me to start studying; Astri and John Leroy, without whom there would have been no Spider Club of southern Africa or source of practical experience in the early days; Linda Duigan, my artist, who can read my mind and see the spiders in my head as I'd like to see them on paper; the late Vince Roth for reading the text and advising on many taxonomic changes; Annette van den Berg, Peter Croeser, Dr Gerry Newlands, Koos de Wet, Dr Joh Henschel and Andrew Smith, for their interest, advice and time spent in teaching; all those members of the Spider Club, especially Steve Langton and Lorenzo Prendini, who have collected and supplied me with specimens to work on; Tracey Groenewald for the hours spent at the photostat machine; and last but not least, my wife Sal, for her patience and encouragement throughout.

REVISION NOTE AND ACKNOWLEDGEMENTS – 2010 EDITION

In October 2002 Martin Filmer signed my copy of Southern African Spiders, with the following inscription: 'For Norman, my student who became my teacher'. Martin sadly passed away on 14 September 2004. He always wanted me to revise his book and in 2009 Pippa Parker asked if I would do the revision. Hope you are happy with the revision, Martin!

The digital age has made working on this book a pleasure. Various researchers have supplied me with reprints of their revisions, either in printed format or PDFs and information on the web. Dr Ansie Dippenaar-Schoeman is thanked for her quick response to all my requests; without her support this revision would be less complete. Dr Lorenzo Prendini, Dr Matjaz Kuntner, Dr Jeremy Miller, Dr Rudy Jocque, Charles Haddad, Leon Lotz, Dr Charles Griswold, Richard Gallon, Dr Tony Russell-Smith, Stefan Foord, Prof Otto Krause, Dr Joh Henschel, Astri Leroy, Ian Engelbrect, Jonathan Leeming and John Visser have all assisted with information and comments. Thanks to Matjaz Kuntner, Jeremy Miller and Dr Joh Henschel for donations of images and Dr Ansie Dippenaar-Schoeman and Dr Rudy Jocque for the use of the illustration of *Calommata simoni* from *African Spiders – An Identification Manual*.

Thanks to the Iziko Museum's Entomology Department, for support and use of their facilities: Dr Hamish Robertson, Dr Simon van Noort, Dawn Larsen and Margie Cochrane. The good people at Struik Nature with whom it was a pleasure to work: Pippa Parker, Joy Clack, Janice Evans, Ian Parsons and Helen de Villiers. To Sally Filmer for passing the bulk of Martin's library on to me. Finally, to my wife Dawn and daughter Nicole for their assistance and for enduring the many hours I spent in my study.

Published by Struik Nature
(an imprint of Penguin Random House (Pty) Ltd)
Company Reg. No. 1953/000441/07
The Estuaries No. 4, Oxbow Crescent,
Century Avenue, Century City, 7441
PO Box 1144, Cape Town, 8000 South Africa

Visit **www.randomstruik.co.za** and join the Struik Nature Club for updates, news, events and special offers.

First published 1991
Second edition 2010

10 9 8 7 6 5 4

Publisher: Pippa Parker
Managing editor: Helen de Villiers
Editors: Tracey Hawthorne (1st edition),
Joy Clack & Ian Parsons (2nd edition)
Designer: Janice Evans
Illustrators: Linda Duigan & Nicole Larsen
Proofreader: Glynne Newlands
Indexer: Cora Ovens

Reproduction by Hirt &
Carter Cape (Pty) Ltd
Printed and bound by Times Offset
(M) Sdn Bhd, Malaysia

ISBN 978 1 77007 801 7 (Print)
ISBN 978 1 43170 182 7 (ePub)
ISBN 978 1 43170 183 4 (ePdf)

CONTENTS

INTRODUCTION

Spiders are, perhaps, among the most misunderstood creatures on earth, and this is due mainly to ignorance. There is no real basis for the fear and dislike many people have of spiders. From childhood, people are taught to kill or avoid spiders because they are 'poisonous'. When you consider that at some stage, most people come into contact with spiders – knowingly or unknowingly – without coming to any harm, it should be clear how erroneous it is to think that all spiders are venomous or dangerous.

Many spiders are minute and, as such, are not easily seen. Some, on the other hand, are veritable giants, but their distribution and lifestyles make them difficult to find as well. By far the greatest majority of spiders encountered are the small- to medium-sized, dull-coloured creatures that wander freely around the home and garden. *Filmer's Spiders: An Identification Guide for Southern Africa* is a guided tour through the colourful spectrum of spiders that live all around us in a myriad habitats.

Spiders belong to the phylum Arthropoda, and this phylum makes up about 80 per cent of all known animals. The word 'arthropod' means 'jointed leg'. Arthropods have an exoskeleton (a hard outer body covering), which includes three or four pairs of legs that are jointed so that they can bend. Arthropoda have been living on earth for literally millions of years.

The major terrestrial arthropod groups consist of the classes Insecta and Arachnida. Insects have three body parts (head, thorax and abdomen) compared to the two in arachnids. Insects have two compound eyes and two

or three simple eyes, antennae and six legs compared to arachnids' eight simple eyes, lack of antennae and eight legs. Insects usually have two or four wings, breathe through tracheae and usually develop through stages of metamorphosis, while arachnids lack wings, breathe using tracheae, book lungs, or both, and do not metamorphose (see p. 8 for typical spider anatomy). Arachnids usually take live prey that is pre-digested outside the body. Insects are more catholic, taking both live and dead prey, or are vegetarian, with digestion taking place internally. Spiders, scorpions, pseudoscorpions and the insect order Hymenoptera (bees, wasps and ants) use venom to catch prey.

Arachnids, those arthropods having eight legs, have been here for about 400 million years, some 150 million years longer than the insects as we know them today. While more than a million species of insect have thus far been described, a mere 40 000 species of spider are known. However, it is estimated that this figure represents less than 30 per cent of those spiders that actually exist, and further collection and identification are required to broaden our knowledge of these fascinating creatures.

There are eleven extant arachnid orders, namely **Acari**, **Amblypygi**, **Araneae**, **Opiliones**, **Palpigradi**, **Pseudoscorpiones**, Ricinulei, **Schizomida**, **Scorpiones**, **Solifugae** and Uropygi. A brief description follows of the common orders that occur in southern Africa (marked in bold). The Araneae, being the focus of this book, are discussed in more detail thereafter.

Acari: This order includes the ticks (soft- and hard-bodied) and mites, ranging in size from less than 1 mm to 20 mm. Acaris differ from other arachnids in that they may have only six legs during the nymphal stage, and that certain groups are parasitic to both invertebrates and vertebrates, being vectors of numerous diseases (including tick-bite fever in humans). *Sarcoptes scabiei* (Scabies mite) is a skin parasite of people and mammals. It must be noted that these often disliked arachnids are important in the biological control of pest arthropods.

Red velvet mite, Trombiculidae *sp.*

Amblypygi: Whip spiders are not spiders at all, but the name is more appropriate than 'whip scorpions'. Four species occur in southern Africa: *Damon annulatipes* (eastern region), *Damon variegatus* (northern region), *Phrynicodamon scullyi* (western region) and *Hemiphrynus machadoi* (northern Namibia). These are broad, dorsoventrally flattened

Whip spider, Phrynicodamon scullyi, *with a whip-like first pair of legs.*

arachnids with raptorial pedipalps (see Anatomy on p. 8) and an extremely elongated first pair of legs used not for walking, but as feelers. Whip spiders usually move sideways and use their sensory legs to feel for prey that is caught with the raptorial pedipalps. These harmless creatures carry their 15–50 eggs inside a ventral membrane. As with scorpions, the young are carried on the back.

Opiliones: Previously known as Phalangida, harvestmen are mainly found terrestrially in moist regions. They have a poor dispersal rate resulting in speciation, with the Cape Peninsula being especially rich in endemic species. They have short, rounded bodies and only two eyes; eyes are absent in cave species. The sub-order Palpitores has long, thin legs, and therefore bears the common name Daddy longlegs. Conversely, the suborder Lanitores has short legs and moves about slowly. Males of this suborder differ from other arachnids in having a penis, as well as accumulating and looking after the eggs of a number of females. Opilions prey on insects and snails and consume dead and vegetable matter.

Harvestmen, of the suborder Palpitores, have long legs.

Palpigradi: The order Palpigradi (micro whip scorpions) is the rarest of all arachnid orders. It consists of only one family. Two species occur in our region, specifically in the Drakensberg and Potchefstroom areas. Micro whip scorpions are very small to small (1–2 mm) and do not have eyes. They occur in moist leaf litter and easily die from desiccation if removed from their habitat.

Pseudoscorpiones: These very small to small (2–5 mm) arachnids are similar to scorpions, hence the name, but lack the typical metasoma (tail) with sting. The palpal chelae possess venom glands, which exit through the upper fixed or lower movable finger. A silk gland with a galea (spinneret) opens on the movable finger. The female uses silk to construct a nesting chamber. Pseudoscorpions have four, two or no eyes and detect prey with cone-like sensory organs and trichobothria (fine sensory setae) on the palpal chelae. They can be found in litter and under rocks or bark, and the females are often carried by other arthropods, mammals or birds. They are harmless, but their venom is effective in prey capture. Pseudoscorpions are most common from KwaZulu-Natal to the Western Cape, with 135 species known.

Scorpiones: These arachnids (ranging from 23–210 mm) are well known and widely feared. Scorpions have three body segments. The prosoma contains the chelicerae, pedipalps with chelae, four pairs of legs and eight or six eyes (two median eyes and two pairs of lateral eyes with either two or three eyes). The opisthosoma is divided into a broad anterior mesosoma and a slender distal caudal segment, the metasoma, which bears the sting. There are four families in southern Africa, but only three are commonly encountered, namely the Buthidae, Scorpionidae and Liochelidae

families. The Buthidae family, recognized by its slender pedipalps and thick tail, contains some of the world's most dangerous scorpions. These thick-tailed scorpions swing their stingers in all directions, unlike the thin-tailed families, and thus can sting more easily. *Parabuthus granulatus* and *P. transvaalicus* are two species whose stings can result in death. In southern Africa, the Scorpionidae family is represented

The scorpion-like Pseudoscorpion.

Parabuthus granulatus, *our most lethal scorpion.*

A burrowing scorpion, Opistophthalmus austerus, *with distinctive palpal chelae.*

by the genus *Opistophthalmus*, recognized by its thin tail and a large pair of palpal chelae. These burrowing scorpions have weaker venom and need to hold onto prey or even crush their prey to death. They sting over the body and can therefore easily be picked up by hand – at your own peril. The Liochelidae family (previously Ischnuridae) has three genera. They are more flattened and have very thin tails. *Hadogenes* (rock scorpions) are found from the Cederberg northwards; their koppie habitat is under siege in the area, as it is being plundered for building materials. *Opisthacanthus* occurs outside of arid areas, usually in trees or under rocks in forests. *Cheloctonus* is a genus with one species occurring in the northeastern parts of southern Africa, and is similar to *Opisthacanthus*. Liochelids are harmless and do not easily sting.

A ferocious-looking nocturnal Solifuge.

The diurnal Solifuge is more colourful.

Solifugae: The name of the Solifuge originates from the Latin 'to flee from the sun'; appropriately, most species are nocturnal. These apparently ferocious 'hairy' arachnids are much feared, but are completely harmless, as they possess no venom. They are known by various common names, including: sun spider, wind scorpion, red roman, camel spider, jerrymander, roman spider, and the Afrikaans terms *jagspinnekop*, *haarskeerder* and *baardskeerder*. The two latter names imply that they cut hair – although they have no apparatus capable of doing so. These 10–70 mm arachnids have enormous forward-projecting chelicerae armed with teeth. The upper jaw is fixed, while the lower jaw is movable (similar to the pedipalps of scorpions). Males can easily be distinguished from females by their flangella (similar to swept-back aerials). The first legs are shortest and are used as sensory organs. The other three pairs increase in length to the fourth (longest) pair, and are used for running. Solifuges have only two median eyes (the lateral eyes are vestigial or entirely absent), and rely on tactile senses for prey capture. The pedipalps, which are longer than the legs, are held forward to detect prey with their many trichobothria, and terminate in adhesive organs. These suction organs allow solifuges to catch prey and climb smooth surfaces, and aid in drinking water. The prosoma and opisthosoma are segmented. The fourth pair of legs has racquet organs that function as chemoreceptors.

Araneae: This is the second largest arachnid order of arachnida, ranking seventh in total species diversity out of all animal orders. Spiders are found in every part of the world (excluding Antarctica). They are small creatures with two main body parts, eight jointed legs, external skeletons and two to eight simple eyes. They produce silk, which they put to use in a variety of specialized ways.

The anatomy of a spider

Arachnids, unlike insects, have only two main body parts, the cephalothorax and the abdomen. All arachnids have eight legs. Their mandibles (known as chelicerae) are modified for seizing and grasping. Spiders differ from other arachnids in that the abdomen is not segmented and is joined to the cephalothorax by a narrow segment, the pedicel. (The scientific name for the cephalothorax, which provides attachments for the four pairs of legs, the chelicerae and the pedipalps, is the prosoma, while the abdomen is known as the opisthosoma.)

THE CEPHALOTHORAX (PROSOMA)

Like the abdomen, the cephalothorax is unsegmented, but it bears evidence of its ancestry in the form of a thoracic groove demarcating the head area. In many spiders, this groove is difficult to detect and is mentioned here only to give location to the head area. The head area houses the eyes, the chelicerae and the mouthparts of the spider. The eyes are simple ocelli and are usually situated at the front of the head area, often on a slightly raised protuberance. The usual number of eyes is eight, but there are species with just two, four or six eyes; some cave spiders have no eyes at all. The eyes may be set in one, two or three rows and may be of the same size or unequal in size. In a typical spider with eight eyes set in two rows of four, we can distinguish the anterior median eyes (the two middle front eyes), the anterior lateral eyes (the two outer front eyes), the posterior median eyes (the two middle back eyes) and the posterior lateral eyes (the two outer back eyes).

Often, the anterior median eyes are larger than the other eyes (as in the family Salticidae, but not in the Deinopidae or Lycosidae).

DORSAL VIEW OF SPIDER

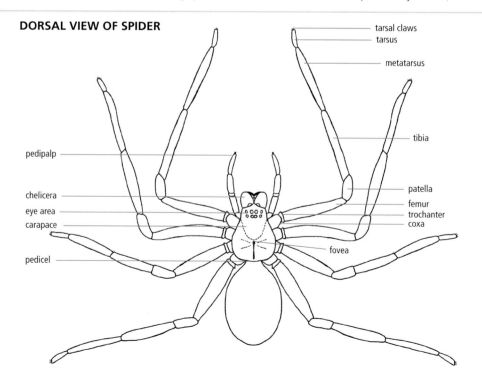

EYE PATTERNS

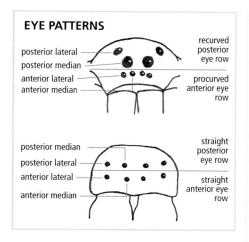

THE FACE

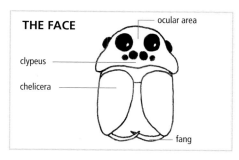

eyes are further forward than the median eyes), they are said to be procurved; if they are curved towards the back, they are said to be recurved. When the curvature is great, the posterior median eyes are widely separated and the posterior lateral eyes are set far back on the carapace (the dorsal part of the cephalothorax), the eyes are said to be in three rows. This arrangement of eyes is typical of certain genera of the family Lycosidae. The area containing the two rows of eyes is

Irrespective of size, they are always the 'main' eyes and differ in structure and development from the subsidiary eyes. Because they lack a reflective layer, they always appear black. The rows of eyes are frequently curved. If they are curved forward (that is, the lateral

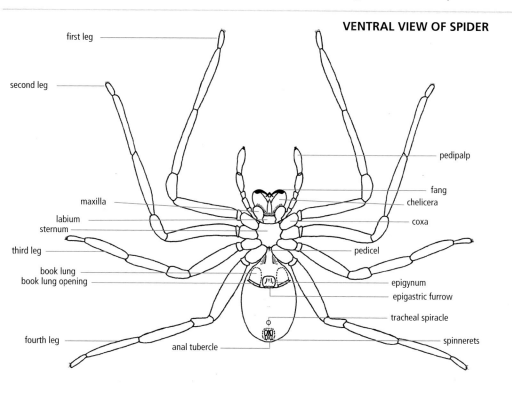

VENTRAL VIEW OF SPIDER

known as the ocular area; the area between the anterior eye row and the margin of the chelicerae is known as the clypeus; and the part of the head that is visible when the spider is seen from the front is known as the face.

The chelicerae, in front of and above the mouthparts, are the first pair of appendages of the cephalothorax. They consist of two sections: a large basal section and a smaller articulated fang. The fang can fold down into a groove in the basal section, which may have teeth-like spines, known as cheliceral teeth, on both sides. Spiders with such spines are able to crush their prey into an unrecognizable mass. Spiders without these spines suck up their liquefied prey through small bite holes in the prey. The chelicerae also allow spiders to grasp and transport prey, carry the egg sac (as in the Scytodidae) and dig burrows (as in the Ctenizidae); and, in some of the small linyphiids, the chelicerae are equipped with stridulatory organs.

When spiders attack, they raise their fangs and hold them outwards, following the contour of the basal section. When the fangs penetrate the prey, the venom is injected through small apertures at the fang tips. In the mygalomorphs, the fangs strike forwards and downwards, and are known as paraxial fangs. In the so-called true spiders, the araneomorphs, fangs strike towards each other and are known as diaxial fangs.

The spider's mouth is a cavity situated between the pedipalps, the maxillae of which form the sides of the mouth. These maxillae are covered with fine hairs (the scopulae), which assist in filtering out any small particles of cuticle from the crushed prey. Spiders digest their food outside their bodies by injecting into their prey – along with the venom – special enzymes that break up and liquefy the body contents of the prey.

Those spiders without cheliceral teeth suck up the liquefied contents, leaving a perfect shell of the victim.

The labium forms the bottom part of the mouth. It is a thickened sclerite, which is movable to a lesser or greater degree (although sometimes not at all).

The pedipalps are the second pair of appendages of the cephalothorax. Unlike the legs, the pedipalps consist of only six segments, the metatarsus being absent. Also, there is never more than one tarsal claw on a pedipalp. In females, the pedipalps are simple structures, but in male spiders, the tarsus is highly modified for use in mating. The pedipalp of the male is of special importance to taxonomists, as it is unique to each species of spider. Spiders with relatively simple pedipalps are known as haplogyne spiders, while spiders with highly complex pedipalps are known as entelegyne spiders.

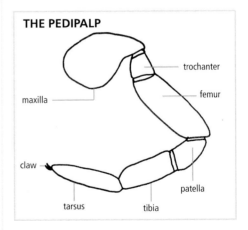

THE PEDIPALP

- trochanter
- femur
- maxilla
- claw
- patella
- tarsus
- tibia

The thorax area of the cephalothorax bears the four pairs of jointed legs. The plate forming the ventral wall of the thorax is called the sternum and, like the carapace, it is hardened and stiff. It occupies the entire space between the four pairs of legs.

The legs of the spider are jointed and connect to the cephalothorax along the pliable connection between the carapace and the sternum. Each leg consists of seven segments: the coxa, a short, thickened base attached to the body of the spider; the trochanter, a second shortened articulation; the femur, which is long; the patella, acting as a knee joint; the tibia, which like the femur is long but is more slender; the metatarsus; and the tarsus, to which are attached two or three claws. Attached to the tarsi of many spiders are numerous scopulae, looking rather like tufts. The tips of these hairs spread out to form end feet. The literally thousands of end feet allow spiders to cling to smooth surfaces by means of friction. The lower surfaces of the tarsus and metatarsus are also often clothed in scopulae.

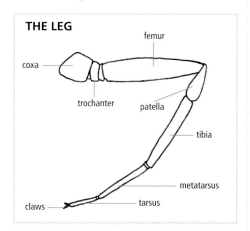

THE LEG

femur

coxa

trochanter

patella

tibia

metatarsus

claws

tarsus

All spiders have eight jointed legs, but how different these legs can be is a source of amazement: from long, delicate legs to short, fat, stubby ones, and all designed for the specific spider's living habits. Web-bound spiders, for example, are generally clumsy away from their silken homes, while hunting spiders would become horribly tangled if they tried to traverse a web.

Apart from providing the spider with a means of locomotion, the legs are equipped with a variety of sensory organs that allow the spider to monitor its environment. Some, such as the articulated setae, function as mechanoreceptors, monitoring touch and vibration. Others are more highly refined, such as the trichobothria (very fine setae set at right angles to the leg surface in a circular surround of cuticle), which react to minute air currents and very low-frequency sounds. At the leg joints are slit sensilla mechanoreceptors known as lyriform organs, which measure the stress in the surrounding cuticle. Also at the joints are chemoreceptors in the form of open-ended setae that expose the nerve fibres to the environment; chemosensitive setae; and spherical pits in the dorsal surface of each tarsus known as the tarsal organs.

Spiders that spin cribellate silk (silk emanating from the cribellum, a specialized spinning organ) have, on the margin of the metatarsus of the fourth leg, one or two rows of curved spines (known as the calamistrum), which allow them to 'comb out' the cribellate silk.

THE ABDOMEN (OPISTHOSOMA)

In spiders the abdomen is unsegmented and usually soft and sac-like. The pedicel, through which the blood vessels, nerves and intestine pass, joins the abdomen to the cephalothorax. This slender stem is often overlooked, as the bulbous abdomen overhanging the carapace usually conceals it. However, in the more delicate spiders and those mimicking insects, the pedicel is quite easily discernible. The dorsal aspect of the abdomen often shows a set of four or more indentations, which indicate the internal muscle attachment points. These points and the variations in patterns and colours on the abdomen are often of help in identifying a family, genus or species. Of more importance anatomically – especially for the taxonomist – is the ventral aspect of the abdomen.

Lying directly behind the pedicel is the epigastrium, which is often more rounded than the rear part of the abdomen. Sometimes hardened, it occupies about one third of the abdomen and ends in an epigastric furrow. The opening for the reproductive organs is centred along this furrow, and at each end is an opening for the book lungs. In spiders having four book lungs, the remaining openings occur on the more central portion of the abdomen. Situated along the midline but towards the spinnerets are the tracheal spiracles, which are additional respiratory organs.

The reproductive opening in the male is small and simple, serving only to emit sperm, which is then manually transmitted to the pedipalps. In the mature female, the reproductive opening, the epigynum, opens to the two internal ovaries. The outer configuration of the epigynum, which may be very complicated, is of importance to the taxonomist in identifying spiders to species level, and is chitinous in entelegyne spiders.

The spinnerets are grouped in pairs at the rear ventral part of the abdomen. There may

COLULUS

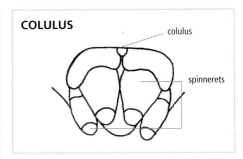

be two, four or six spinnerets, identified as anterior, median or posterior as they lie from the front to the back of the abdomen. In some spiders, there is a specialized spinning organ known as the cribellum. In others, the colulus (pictured above) is an evolutionary remnant of the cribellum. (The spinnerets and silk production are discussed fully on pp. 20–25.)

The anal tubercle is situated above the posterior spinnerets.

Reproduction and growth

COURTSHIP AND MATING

When it comes to reproduction, most people would say, 'I'm glad I'm not a spider!' Spiders have earned a reputation for cannibalism following mating, and arachnid reproduction can indeed be dangerous for the male, and is also highly complex – both in the courtship phase and in the actual mating process.

Unique to spiders is the modification of the male pedipalps as organs of reproduction. As remarkable is the fact that the female epigynum is so constructed as to accept only the configuration of her conspecific male's pedipalp. This 'lock-and-key' mechanism ensures that there can be no species mixing. (Spider taxonomists rely almost entirely on the shape and configuration of the sexual organs to identify different species.)

CRIBELLUM

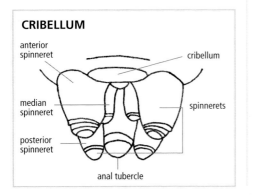

Immature spiders are, for all practical purposes, sexless. In immature males, the pedipalps are nonfunctional, as is the epigynum in immature females. These develop into functional reproductive organs at the time of the final ecdysis (shedding of the hard exoskeleton) into adulthood. Once fully mature, the male's single aim in life is to find a female with which to mate.

Before courting begins, the male's pedipalps have to be charged with seminal fluid. In both males and females, the genital pore is situated on the ventral side of the abdomen, between the book lungs. To transfer sperm from this pore to the palps, the male spider first spins a sperm web (a small, triangular or square web) just above the substrate. Straddling the web, he deposits a drop of sperm at its centre. The spider then either dips his palps into the sperm or presses his palps up against the sperm from the underside of the web. Similar to an old-fashioned fountain pen, the embolus (the sex organ situated at the end of the pedipalp) draws up the fluid.

N Larsen

The male Thomisus *sits on the female's abdomen and will mate when she moults into an adult.*

The female spider lives a solitary life devoted to catching prey and feeding. Whatever moves in her vicinity, she will attack and either kill or drive off. As a result, male spiders have evolved a complex and amazing variety of courtship rituals, only a few of which are described here. There are two main approaches, and these are based on the visual ability of the particular species. Long-sighted spiders are mainly diurnal maters, while short-sighted ones will mate at any time.

Once a female has been located, it is up to the male to convince her that he is a male of her species and that she should succumb to his advances. In the families Lycosidae and Salticidae, which have good vision, the males carry out an elaborate courtship dance. The lycosid male waves his pedipalps up and down in rhythmic movements while tapping the front pair of legs on the substrate. He moves slowly towards the female, awaiting a signal that she is ready to accept him and that she will not attack. There may be some leg touching and rubbing before actual mating takes place. Some salticid males are adorned with elaborate hairs – often brightly coloured – on their pedipalps. Waving these, with the first pair of front legs raised high above his head, the spider moves in an arc around the female, waiting for her signal of acceptance. On the other hand, those spiders with poor vision do not have an elaborate courtship dance, and may indulge in no more than some leg tickling before mating occurs.

For most web-building spiders, courtship is purely a tactile affair, with the male coming to the edge of the web and plucking or tapping on the silken strands to announce his presence. Some araneid males are much smaller than their mates, and in *Argiope* the female can weigh up to a thousand times as much as the male. Obviously, the *Argiope* male has to be extra careful to avoid becoming a meal! In some of the larger araneid species, the male approaches the female's web and tweaks the strand on which she is sitting. Invariably, he has to drop down on a drag line to avoid her initial rush forwards to attack, before clambering back up to the web and trying again… and again and again and again!

Once the female is convinced that her suitor is a prospective mate and not prey, the male spins a special mating thread. He proceeds to lure the female onto this thread with more plucking and tweaking movements. Female araneid ardour is not long-lasting and once mating has occurred, the male has to beat a fast retreat or suffer being eaten. (Many spider genera do have much less complex and far more civilized mating procedures, however.)

The males of some spider families (for example, the theridiids and linyphiids) are equipped with a stridulatory organ. Once on the female's web, the male spider may stridulate, which causes a high-pitched vibration. The sound not only brings the female out into the open, but renders her receptive to the male's approach.

The act of copulation can last from seconds to hours, depending on the species. In some, the courtship is greatly extended and the mating very brief, while in others there may be hardly any courtship, while mating may last up to seven hours. The male inserts his pedipalps one at a time (or in the case of some of the more primitive spiders, both at once) into the female's epigynum and thus transfers the sperm to her.

Some spiders (such as species of the families Dictynidae, Eresidae and Agelenidae) do live a social life of sorts, the sexes cohabiting more or less amicably in the female's web. Other female spiders eat their mates during or after copulation. This often has to do with the manner in which the male approaches the female, and the position he adopts for mating. The most notorious spouse-eating spider is *Latrodectus*, whose antisocial behaviour has earned it the common name 'Black widow spider'.

There are some rather amusing methods that male spiders use to avoid falling prey to their prospective mates. The male of some of the pisaurid species catches a fly and neatly enswathe it in silk; then, holding the wrapped gift in his chelicerae, he approaches the female. Once she has accepted it and has started eating it, he nips around and proceeds to mate with her. The males of some of the crab spiders are tiny in comparison to their mates. To overcome his size disadvantage, the male casts strands of silk to and fro across the

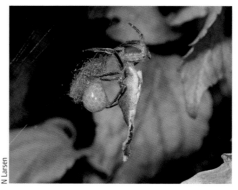

Arachnura constructing an egg sac.

Arachnura laying eggs.

female's abdomen while she is lying in wait for prey, tying her down like the Lilliputians tied down Gulliver. Once she is secured in this way, he mates with her and then leaves her to her own devices. She may take several hours to extricate herself.

Once inseminated, the female may hold the sperm in her spermathecae for days or even months, using only the amount needed to fertilize the eggs she lays at any one time. She is thus able to lay a number of egg sacs full of fertile eggs after only one mating. Araneomorph spiders do not ecdyse after maturing and retain viable sperm for the next egg-laying. Mygalomorph spiders, however, are evaginated during ecdysis and so are rendered virginal after each moult, making it necessary for them to mate again to lay fertile eggs. Gestation periods differ greatly between species and are related to the spiders' lifespans.

Generally, the smaller the spider the fewer eggs it lays in each egg sac, but many of the smaller species make more than one egg sac at a time or over a period of time. Larger spiders tend to make one large egg sac containing a large number of eggs. The number of shapes and sizes of egg sac is legion, and spiders use many methods of camouflage to hide them.

Argiope australis *egg sac situated among vegetation.*

Some spiders, such as the sparassids and the oxyopids, stay with the egg sac and guard it until the young hatch. Some, such as the pisaurids, provide a nursery in which the spiderlings may live in safety until they have reached their second or third instar and are able to fend for themselves. Others, such as the lycosids, carry their young around on their backs until they are ready to disperse.

Arachnura covering her egg sac.

Spiderlings of Argiope australis *soon after emerging from their egg sac.*

GROWTH AND DISPERSAL

Spiders emerge from their eggs as carbon copies of their parents. They grow rapidly through a series of ecdyses, developing from one instar to the next, until finally reaching sexual maturity.

Each time the exuviae (old exoskeleton) has been shed, the spider grows rapidly until the new, pliable exoskeleton hardens and effectively halts any further growth. The spider is then obliged to wait for the next ecdysis before growing any bigger. The smaller the spider, the fewer the ecdyses required to attain adulthood. Medium-sized spiders ecdyse approximately seven times, and the larger species up to 10 times. Generally, spiders seek a quiet place to ecdyse, for they are at their most vulnerable during and immediately after moulting.

When still very young, some spiderlings disperse by means of ballooning. They climb

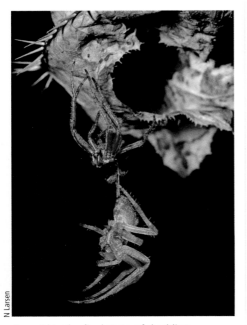

Araneid in the final stage of shedding.

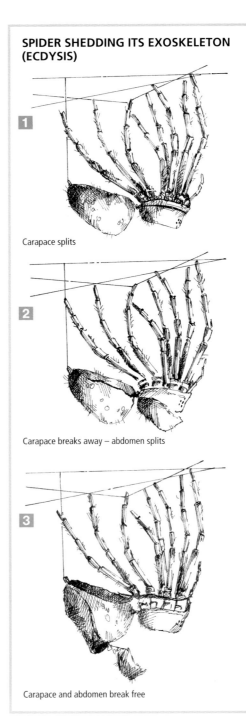

SPIDER SHEDDING ITS EXOSKELETON (ECDYSIS)

1 Carapace splits

2 Carapace breaks away – abdomen splits

3 Carapace and abdomen break free

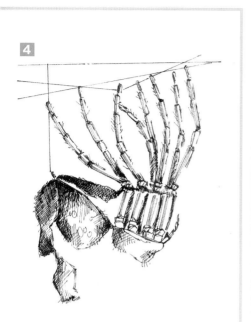

New spider emerges from old skin

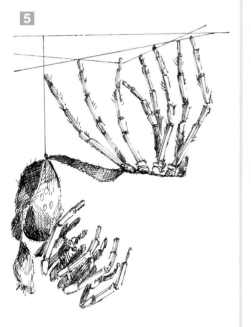

Ecdysis complete – spider flexes new legs

N Larsen

Synema extruding silk from its spinnerets in order to balloon.

up to the highest vantage point they can find (a small tree, maybe a fence post). Then, facing into the wind, they raise their abdomens as high as they can and emit strands of silken thread from their spinnerets. Soon there is enough silk to be carried on the wind, and the spiderling floats away from its birthplace to find a new home. Many of the tiny spiders lose their lives, but sufficient numbers survive to start up colonies elsewhere and spread the species. Spiderlings have landed on the decks of ships thousands of miles from land. In experiments carried out by naturalist/film-maker David Attenborough, ballooning spiders were collected miles above the earth's surface in the upper layers of the stratosphere – none the worse for wear.

By our standards, most spiders live very short lives, growing from spiderlings to adults, then dying, all within one year. Some spiders, especially the mygalomorphs, are known to live in excess of 25 years in captivity, but the majority of the species live for less than 18 months. Male spiders always live shorter lives than females.

Lifestyles and habitats

Eight eyes means four times better vision, right? No, not at all. We cannot really imagine what spiders see, for while we observe our environment primarily with our eyes, most spiders are almost blind. They have to rely on their other senses to keep in touch with the world around them. The wandering hunting spiders do have better vision than their web-bound counterparts, but even they do not rely entirely on their vision. The Salticidae family has the most sophisticated visual apparatus, with the anterior median eyes allowing a degree of binocular vision. This allows spiders in this family to estimate distance – they are able to distinguish objects up to 20 cm.

The key to spiders' senses lies in the sense organs situated on their legs. These organs take the form of various sensory setae and slits in the outer integument of the legs, which allow spiders to sense their immediate environment with great accuracy.

Spiders live everywhere: from the top of the dome of St Paul's Cathedral in London to the stopes of Johannesburg's gold mines; from the blistering heat of the Namib Desert to the frozen northern coasts of Greenland.

The habitat of spiders is almost universal and, as you use this book, you will discover many more places where spiders make their homes. However, using the broad categories described in this section, the families are arranged according to where you are **most likely** to find them. Clearly, there are exceptions to every rule. For example, genera of the orb-web spiders such as *Aethriscus* (the bird-dropping spider) and *Cladomelea* (the bolas spider) do not make webs at all, let alone 'orb' webs. On the whole, every effort has been made to flow from one habitat and lifestyle to the next while retaining some sort of continuity. Within each group, the spider families are listed alphabetically and not according to relationships, and possible variations within any one family will become evident as you use the book to identify spiders.

WEB-BOUND SPIDERS

To most people, a spider is inextricably linked with the concept of a web; and a web, in turn, with an orb web. More than half of all known spiders spin some form of web for prey capture, but only a few of these spin orb webs.

Orb-web spiders

These spiders build their unique structural masterpieces in open spaces between trees, branches of trees or man-made objects such as fence wires. Their webs may vary in size from a few centimetres to a few metres across. The spider sets up home either in the web (usually at the hub) or in a retreat, which is connected to the hub with a signal line. Most orb webs are vertical or built at a slight angle, but some are horizontal, especially those of the Uloboridae family. Some of the families classified as orb-web builders are Araneidae, Nephilidae, Tetragnathidae and Uloboridae. However, some genera within these families do not spin orb webs. For example, *Cladomelea* of the family Araneidae spins a sticky ball on a silken thread (known as a bolas-line), which it whirls around to catch prey.

Cribellate-web spiders

These spiders build orb webs, sheet webs and even nets to capture prey. Their silk has a flocculent (woolly) texture and works on the same principle as Velcro. In this group we have the Amaurobiidae, Phyxelididae, Eresidae, Filistatidae and Uloboridae. The net-throwing spiders of the family Deinopidae use a rete (similar to a gladiator's net) to throw over passing prey.

Tube-web/burrowing spiders

Spiders living in tubes or tunnels in the ground, under stones and rocks, in holes and cracks of trees and in human artifacts such as poles, tins and cracked walls generally line the sides of their abode with a silken sheet, rounding off the entrance with a ridge of silk and debris or closing it with a tight-fitting trapdoor. Often radiating from the entrance is a spiral of signal lines to alert the spider to approaching prey. The members of one family of mygalomorph spiders, the Atypidae, live in an enclosed silken tube for their entire lives. Part of this tube is constructed under the ground, with the section above the ground lying horizontally. The spider lurking within the tube thrusts a pair of long and sharp fangs through the tube wall to catch prey moving over the upper section. Families using tunnel webs include most of the mygalomorph spiders discussed in the second part of the book and, among the araneomorphs, the Amaurobiidae, Phyxelididae, Filistatidae and Segestriidae, and some genera of the Eresidae, Lycosidae and Oecobiidae.

Sheet-web/funnel-web spiders

Sheet webs, as the name implies, look like silken sheets and are usually built close to the substrate, often with a funnel at one end. The web may vary in size from 25 cm in diameter to tiny sheets of less than 1 cm across. These sheet webs house such families as the Agelenidae, Pisauridae, Cyatholipidae, Hahniidae, Oecobiidae and Linyphiidae, and some members of the family Lycosidae.

Cob-web spiders

These spiders build three-dimensional webs, which allow them to capture prey coming from above or below the central section housing the retreat. The family most often associated with this kind of web is the Theridiidae, but the Nesticidae family also builds scaffold webs. Also in this group are the tiny dictynid spiders, the pholcids and the drymusids.

Free-living web invaders

These are spiders that live in the webs of other spiders, feeding on prey remains in the web or preying on the host spider. The tiny silver dew-drop spiders (*Argyrodes*) of the family Theridiidae, and the Mimetidae fall into this group.

GROUND-LIVING SPIDERS

Free-living ground spiders

Smaller than the more sedentary burrow dwellers and both diurnal and nocturnal, these spiders may be seen running freely over all sorts of substrate. Those spiders living near or on water are genera of the families Pisauridae and Lycosidae. Intertidal spiders belong to the families Desidae, Anyphaenidae, Linyphiidae and Hahniidae. Spiders living on, in and around rocks may come from the families Oecobiidae, Hersiliidae, Selenopidae, Ctenidae and Eresidae. Desert spiders belong to the families Sicariidae, Sparassidae, Zodariidae and Eresidae. Spiders found in the disturbed soil in and around termite mounds are members of the family Ammoxenidae. Finally, those living with humans in their homes come mainly from the families Miturgidae, Sparassidae, Agelenidae, Gnaphosidae, Pholcidae, Salticidae and Theridiidae.

Burrow-living spiders

Although a few araneomorphs are regarded as 'burrow-living', they are not confined to these burrows. However, most mygalomorphs can be classified as burrow-living spiders. Some genera of the families Lycosidae, Zodariidae, Sparassidae and Eresidae are araneomorphs and do dig burrows, but they are not necessarily confined to them. They are therefore included under the free-living spiders.

FREE-LIVING ARBOREAL SPIDERS

Arboreal spiders live in or among trees or bushes. Each spider family is uniquely adapted to its chosen way of life. Some (such as members of the families Oxyopidae, Miturgidae and Clubionidae) are agile and leap from leaf to leaf in pursuit of their prey, while others (for example, some genera belonging to the family Thomisidae) spend their entire lives on a single part of the plant.

Many spiders live on the stems and blades of grass. They tend to take on the colour of the grass in which they live and are mostly yellowish-brown to dull green. Ambushers, they cling to the stems, front legs stretched out in front of them as they await their prey. Genera of the families Thomisidae and Philodromidae live in the grass.

The brightly coloured, fat, female crab spiders of the family Thomisidae match the colour of the flower on which they sit. In pinks, yellows, pale greens and white, they wait in ambush for insects visiting the flower for nectar.

Like the grass and flower dwellers, the foliage dwellers vary in colour from fawn to bright green. Free-running and often living their whole lives on one plant, they may move around rapidly or lie in wait and only now and then dash out to attack passing prey. Foliage dwellers include members of the families Oxyopidae, Clubionidae, Sparassidae and Thomisidae.

The bark dwellers tend to be flattened slightly or, as in the family Trochanteriidae, grossly. They vary in colour from grey to dark brown and black. Remaining motionless unless provoked, they can move with incredible speed. Bark dwellers of the families Hersiliidae and Trochanteriidae live entirely on, in or under the living or dead bark of trees. Some bark dwellers (such as genera of the family Araneidae), on the other hand, use the bark of trees as a retreat when not hunting. Others (such as *Caerostris*) camouflage themselves by pulling up their legs against their abdomens to resemble dried-out buds or thorny growths on the tree.

The silk of spiders

All spiders possess silk glands and spinnerets to produce silk threads. Unlike those insects that produce silk only to build cocoons for pupating, spiders – from the first instar – can spin silken threads for a variety of purposes. Silk is a protein, which is produced inside the body of the spider by up to six distinct glands. Each gland produces a specific type of silk, with a special function, but only a few families have all six glands. Most spiders have at least three or four of the six glands.

Tubuliform glands, which are used to produce egg sacs, are found only in female spiders. All spiders, on the other hand, possess aciniform glands. Males need these glands to produce their sperm webs, while females use them to produce silk for the outer egg sacs. Both sexes use them to produce enswathing silk to wrap prey. Spiders not using silk for prey capture lack aggregate glands; these glands are most typical of the orb-web spiders.

Under a microscope, spider silk can be seen to be made up of numerous fine strands – and not just one solid line. (The tensile strength of spider silk exceeds that of high-grade steel!) Each silk gland leads to a spinneret, and each spinneret is made up of numerous tiny spigots. Silk is emitted from the spigots not by muscular pressure, but by the pressure of the silk as it emanates from the glands.

Spiders use silk in many ways: the spider may drop down while producing its silken thread; walk away from a point of attachment while feeding out its silk; pull out the silk with its fourth pair of legs, or eject the silk into the wind as it is about to balloon. The silk does not dry as it comes into contact with the air. Rather, the molecules in the silk align in a specific way, which renders each thread stable and 'dry' as it leaves the spigots.

The eight families of cribellate spider possess an additional spinning organ, the cribellum, which is situated in front of the anterior spinnerets. This oblong, sieve-like plate is a single organ, but may be divided by a keel (or keels) to be a bipartite, tripartite or quadripartite organ. It is fed by up to 40 000 spigots, and the very fine threads emanating from them are combed out into a hackled band by the rhythmic movements of the calamistrum on the spider's fourth legs, rather like teasing your hair with a teasing comb. Cribellate silk contains no viscid silk such as that produced by the aggregate glands, and operates much as Velcro does.

Ground-living or plant-living spiders mostly make use of attachment discs, drag lines, enswathing silk and a mating web for reproduction, but species of the web-bound spiders may make use of all six glands. For example, *Araneus*, with its well-known wagon-wheel web, spins every kind of silk to meet the needs of its everyday life.

Some web-bound spiders (which use their webs, of whatever construction, to catch prey) use their silk to line their abodes. These spiders most often construct a tunnel or burrow, or make their homes in a crack or crevice. While the silk itself is not always used to catch prey, in many cases it is used to construct trip lines. These lines radiate from the entrance of the burrow and relay the movements of approaching prey to the spider waiting at the entrance.

Sheet webs, as made by the families Agelenidae, Pisauridae and Linyphiidae, are easily recognized, especially in the early morning when the dew has settled on them. They provide the spider with a retreat or living area, catch threads to knock down prey and an open, sheet-like plain over which the spider can run to catch prey.

Like sheet webs, scaffold webs (so called because of their appearance) have catch threads. On sheet webs, however, there are catch threads above and below the main frame, lying with and attached to the mooring threads that hold the whole web together. The

SILK GLANDS AND THE FUNCTIONS OF SILK		
GLAND	**FUNCTION**	**SPINNERETS USED**
Ampullate glands	Drag lines and frame threads	Anterior and median
Piriform glands	Attachment discs	Anterior
Aciniform glands	Enswathing silk, sperm webs and the outer walls of egg sacs	Median and posterior
Tubuliform glands	Egg sacs	Median and posterior
Aggregate glands	Glue of sticky spirals	Posterior
Flagelliform glands	Axial threads of sticky spiral	Posterior

threads above the frame serve as knockdown lines, while those attached to the substrate are studded with sticky silken droplets to ensnare crawling or jumping insects.

Specialized webs, such as the rete web of the family Deinopidae and the bolas of the family Araneidae (genus *Cladomelea*), are discussed in full under those families.

Constructing an orb web

Orb webs are widely considered to be the standard spider's web. Whatever the spider, wherever the habitat, most people, if asked to draw 'the spider's home', would draw an orb web. The main family of orb-web spiders is the Araneidae, but other families that build orb webs include the Tetragnathidae and Nephilidae, and some of the genera within the cribellate spider family Uloboridae.

The construction of the web (often a daily occurrence, as the spider puts up the web at dusk only to dismantle it at dawn) follows certain steps.

The bridge

The first step in constructing an orb web is to construct a bridge line. This line may span a considerable distance. The spider sits at a point near to where the web is to be built and spins a number of silken threads, allowing the wind to direct their path to another attachment point (illustrated opposite). The spider then crosses backwards and forwards on the line, laying down additional threads to reinforce the bridge line. Alternatively, the spider starts at a point and walks across the substrate, letting out a drag line. When the spider finds a suitable attachment point, the drag line is pulled up to form a bridge line.

N Larsen

Orb web and retreat of Stone nest spider.

CONSTRUCTING AN ORB WEB

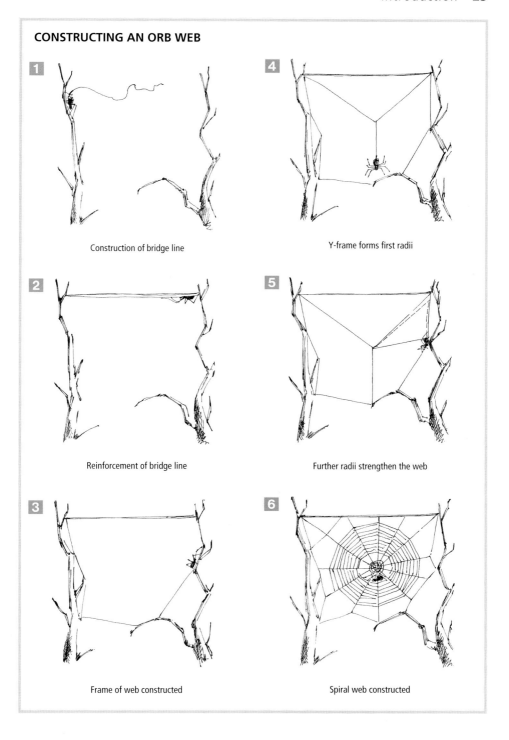

1 Construction of bridge line

2 Reinforcement of bridge line

3 Frame of web constructed

4 Y-frame forms first radii

5 Further radii strengthen the web

6 Spiral web constructed

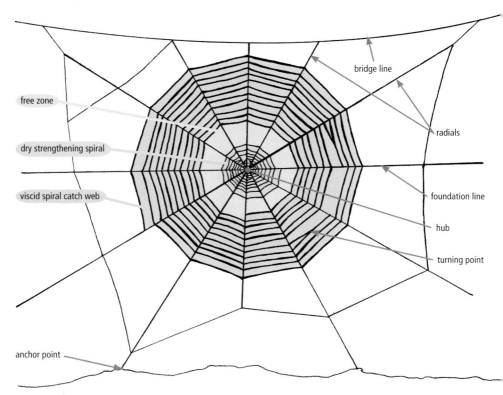

A typical orb web, showing different areas of the web.

The foundation lines

Once the bridge has been reinforced, the spider moves to a second point, lower down, throwing out a drag line behind it, and attaches this to a suitable point with an attachment disc. The spider repeats this step at various points, moving downwards, across and back up to the opposite side of the bridge line. In this way, the spider constructs the 'frame' or foundation lines within which the orb will be made.

The radii

Yet another line is stretched across the bridge line, and the spider takes up a position at the middle of this thread. The spider draws it downwards, to where the centre of the web will be, then continues downwards on one strand to the first available attachment point, where it secures the thread with an attachment disc. Within the framework is now a 'Y' of silken thread. These three threads make up the first radii, and around these the spider continues to make further radii at regular intervals.

The hub

The hub is the centre of the web, where the radii converge. The spider may strengthen it with a mesh of silken threads, reinforce it with a network of crisscross patterns, or leave it open. Some species extend the hub in the form of a stabilimentum (a crisscrossing of strong silk), which radiates outwards horizontally, vertically, or in the form of an 'X'.

The dry-silk zone

Moving outwards from the hub, the spider constructs a varying number of spirals with 'dry' (not sticky) silk. The spider attaches the radii at right angles, drawing them together in even lengths for perhaps six to twelve circles.

The catch-web or viscid zone

Starting from an external point on the frame, the spider spins a viscid thread of silk while moving along and eating the dry, temporary spiral in closely arranged spirals up to the outer edge of the free zone (that area where no spirals will be constructed). Most species take up a position in the middle of the hub (hanging head down, waiting for prey to fly into the web); some wait on the periphery; and others build a signal line to detect prey caught in the web.

The signal line

Signal-line builders build their retreats above and to the side of their webs. This retreat connects to the hub with a sturdy thread, allowing the spider to move freely between the open web and the hidden retreat. It also serves to alert the spider to struggling, ensnared prey.

The stabilimentum

Various theories have been put forward as to the real function of the stabilimenta that some species of orb-web spider construct. The most accepted theories include that it serves as a strengthening mechanism; a warning to large flying insects or birds that may destroy the web if they hit it; and a place to weave in debris and prey remains, among which the spider can conceal itself. Research has shown that the stabilimentum reflects ultraviolet light, which may attract insects into the web.

Orb web without a free zone and with a missing section where prey was caught.

A note on venom

All spiders (bar the Uloboridae) possess venom glands, but not all spiders are harmfully venomous. A few species may be referred to as potentially venomous to humans, but you would have to eat a spider and suffer the symptoms of poisoning from its body contents to be 'poisoned' by it. Apart from the fact that most spiders are so small that their chelicerae cannot pierce human skin, those species that can are most often loath to do so. They would all rather run and hide than confront so large an aggressor.

A pair of venom glands is situated in the cephalothorax. Each gland consists of a sac-like section in which the venom is stored and a long, tapering duct section, which terminates at the tip of the fang as a minute opening. Surrounding the gland are striated muscles that contract, ejecting the venom through the duct.

As is the case with snake bites, a number of factors influence the severity of a spider bite:
1. the amount of venom the spider is able to inject;
2. the site of the bite (a bite on the face has a greater effect than one on the foot); and
3. the age and health of the victim, as well as any personal allergies the victim may have.

Spiders potentially venomous to humans have typically two types of venom: neurotoxic and cytotoxic. Neurotoxic venom affects the neuromuscular synapses and causes heart palpitations, dyspnoea (difficult breathing), raised blood pressure, severe pains in the chest and abdomen, and a condition of extreme fear and anxiety. Only one family, Theridiidae (genus *Latrodectus*), is of medical importance and warrants immediate medical attention. The bite of spiders with neurotoxic venom is extremely painful.

Cytotoxic venom affects the cellular tissue around the site of the bite and, in some instances, tissue throughout the body. The bite is usually painless and the first symptom may simply be a raised red bump, rather like that of a mosquito bite. Severe symptoms develop slowly, the bump becoming painful, then ulcerating into a large surface lesion, which may cover up to 10 cm in diameter. These types of lesion are encountered when the spider is from the families Sicariidae (genus *Loxosceles*) or Miturgidae (genus *Cheiracanthium*). Not well documented in man but proved in animal tests, the venom of *Sicarius*, family Sicariidae, is the most virulent cytotoxin we know of in the region. It causes tissue damage at all levels throughout the body.

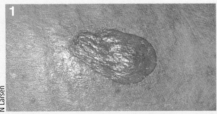

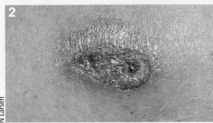

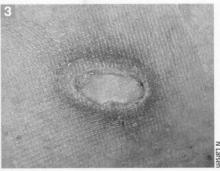

Three healing stages of a Violin spider (genus Loxosceles) *bite: (1) initial blister, (2) necrosis and finally (3) the healing stage. This spider's cytotoxic venom causes an ulcerating wound, which may leave a marked scar.*

N Larsen

Collecting spiders

Conservative estimates put global arachnological fauna at some 523 000 spiders per arable acre of land. While it is indefensible to kill spiders wantonly, you will not necessarily denude the population by collecting them live or preserving them in alcohol. Rather, you are adding to current knowledge, expanding the collections and helping our professionals. Specimens should be labelled with the information listed below.

- **Locality:** *Note where the specimen was collected; include map references if possible and always write down the name of the province.*
- **Date:** *Make a note of when the specimen was collected.*
- **Habitat:** *Include a short description of the specimen's immediate surroundings; for example, if it was taken from a web, from under a stone or from the bark of a tree.*
- **Name:** *Write down your name.*
- **Family:** *Make a tentative identification, if possible.*

NOTE

Baboon spiders (Theraphosids) are protected by law and a permit is required to collect, transport and possess them.

N Larsen

Using a sweep net to sample the grass for spiders.

It is true that some of the larger genera of spiders can be identified in the field; indeed, the large *Nephila* genus can be identified to species level with the naked eye. However, most of the spiders you collect will need to be studied under a magnifying glass or microscope from the top, the bottom and often other angles. This is impossible with the spider running to and fro in the bottle. A dead, wet specimen may be viewed at leisure, as often as is required.

Be aware: 'shapes and sizes' is the name of the game regarding both the spiders themselves and the webs in which you may find them. So often the spider is missed in a web where it may be hiding among the debris of old prey, or it may be crouching in a retreat above the web; the web may be overlooked because it appears as a broken remnant of a once-full orb web. Look, examine and be patient.

The quickest and easiest way of collecting spiders is by means of a sweep net (although some collectors prefer to use a beating tray or net). Professional arachnologists use sweep nets to sample specific sections of grassland within certain defined areas. They sweep the demarcated area at different times of the year to monitor spider populations.

A sweep net may be made from a landing net commonly used by fishermen. Remove the netting and replace it with some sturdy white material such as thick linen, which should be at least twice as deep as the frame of the net is wide. Do not use coloured or patterned materials, as these render small spiders almost impossible to see. If possible, buy a fish net that has a solid, round, metal frame and a removable, screw-in aluminium handle. This will give you two nets in one: a sweep net and a beating net.

Collecting spiders involves sweeping through tall grass and bushes with the net to pick up small to medium-sized spiders of many varieties. Unscrew the handle, hold the net section under the branch of a tree (or the small branches of a bush) and beat the foliage with the handle to knock down spiders living among the leaves and branches. The sweep net can also be used to collect ground dwellers. Simply gather up a wad of leaf litter, spread it out onto the sweep net and sift through it. Many small spiders are found in this way. Real enthusiasts will even use a sieve to get rid of the larger leaves first before sifting through the debris.

After you have collected the specimens, transfer them to a kill bottle, or to an aerated bottle if you want to keep them alive.

N Larsen

Demonstrating the use of a beating net.

N Larsen

A collector using a pooter.

Many families of spider may be collected by the simple hand-to-jar method. Place a wide-mouthed bottle next to the spider and coax the spider into it using a probe of some kind, such as a twig. Although there are only a few medically dangerous spiders, all spiders can bite. 'Hand-to-jar' does not mean physically handling the specimen, especially when dealing with one of the more venomous species. Orb-web spiders are most easily found by walking towards the sun early in the morning or just before sundown. In the morning, you will have the added advantage of glistening dew highlighting the silken threads; and you will be able to spot the sheet webs of the agelenid and linyphiid spiders more easily. Under fallen trees and rocks – and often under debris such as building material – you can find a myriad spider species that can be collected hand-to-jar.

In among leaf litter on the forest floor live some minute spiders, best collected with a tullgren funnel. A wad of leaves is placed in a wide-mouthed funnel, the base of which has been covered with a coarse sieve. The tube of the funnel is placed in a container (for example, an old tin) into which some alcohol has been poured. The tiny spiders make their way through the litter and down the tube, where they fall into the alcohol. (A bright lamp positioned over the funnel will drive some spiders down more quickly, as the leaf-litter dwellers always avoid bright light.) Alternatively, you could leave out the alcohol and collect the spiders live. If you opt to do this, remember to check the funnel regularly, otherwise you will be left with only one spider in the trap – the biggest, which will have eaten all the others!

Another technique for catching ground dwellers is the ground trap or pitfall trap. A medium-sized plastic potting container is set into the ground so that the top is flush with ground level. A funnel made of an old X-ray plate (or some other stiff, slippery material such as smooth cardboard or thick plastic) is placed in the pot. The trap is covered with a large, flat stone or piece of tin and propped up with small stones to keep out predators and the rain. Any unsuspecting spider walking into the funnel will slide down and into the container. The trap may be left dry, and live specimens collected regularly, or alcohol may be placed in a container within the pot to kill and preserve specimens. The trap may then be left unattended and cleaned out once a week.

A pooter or a small brush may be used to suck or dislodge small spiders from rock faces or household walls. A pooter can be made by using rubber tubing, a collecting bottle, a small piece of gauze and some glue or silicone sealant. The spider is covered with the longer tube while you give a short, sharp suck on the shorter tube (see photo on p. 29). The spider is drawn into the collecting bottle, but prevented from being sucked into the mouth by the gauze affixed to the sucking tube.

Tunnel dwellers may be extricated by digging, but this is best left to those collectors who know how to do it without endangering the occupant at the bottom of the tunnel. Join your local spider club or society and go along on outings with experienced collectors.

Many spiders are collected more easily at night, using a headlamp. Spiders' eyes (such as lycosids, sparassids, miturgids and pisaurids) reflect in the light, and the spider may be approached and trapped in a collecting bottle.

Finally, there is the tree trap, which is a strip of corrugated cardboard wrapped around the trunk of a tree and secured with sturdy string or wire. Spiders living on the tree will use the cavities made by the corrugations as retreats, and if the trap is left for two to three weeks, quite a number of interesting spiders may be caught.

A live specimen can be kept in a reasonably small bottle, providing the lid is perforated. If it is not possible to transfer the spider to a larger container within a few days, a small wad of damp cotton wool should be placed in the bottle, as live spiders require a constant supply of water. In large cages it is best to place the water in a shallow dish. If the spider is particularly small, a length of wool can be inserted through one of the holes in the lid and wetted from the outside. Water will then become available to the spider inside without any possibility of waterlogging the container.

The best medium for preserving spiders is 70 per cent alcohol. The spider may be put directly into the alcohol; apart from losing some of its colour, it will be preserved indefinitely. Large spider specimens left for 10 to 12 weeks in alcohol in a refrigerator can be set out with entomological pins on polystyrene. The alcohol will preserve the spider, while the refrigeration will prevent certain of the enzymes in the abdomen from destroying the soft tissues. This will prevent the abdomen from shrivelling as the spider dries out. To display the specimen, apply a small quantity of cold glue to its feet and encase it in a transparent container.

N Larsen

Night collecting with the help of a headlamp.

How to use this book

This identification guide will enable you to identify spiders to family level and, in some cases, to genus or even species level. Pages 18–20 describe how the different families have been grouped – according to habitat and lifestyle. Within each habitat, the resident spider families are discussed, followed by the subfamilies and/or genera within those families. For instance, all the orb-web spiders have been placed in one group, and sheet-web spiders in another. As a result, the first step in identifying a spider is to determine the spider's habitat. Photographs throughout the text help to identify spiders to family level.

Other aspects that can aid identification are anatomy, reproduction and growth, lifestyle and silk. It is important to read the sections on these topics (see pp. 8–25) in order to make sense of the spider descriptions. When attempting to identify a spider, note the size and structure of the web, shape and colour of egg sacs, movement, colour of silk, and prominent physical characteristics. In some cases – where, for example, the spider mimics another animal or where the male is equipped with spurs, special setae or modified palps – it can be almost impossible to identify a specimen without the aid of a microscope and, possibly, professional help. If this is the case, collect the specimen and send it to one of the contacts listed on p. 124.

At the back of the book, the glossary provides definitions for technical terms as they are used throughout the book. This is followed by a list of useful contacts and further reading, which may come in handy as you pursue your interest in spiders.

Only a small percentage of venomous spiders are harmful to humans. Of the 2 000 species of spider that have been identified in southern Africa, only five or six are of medical importance, and another handful are of only minor consequence (see Venom, p. 26). Medically important spiders are indicated with a skull-and-crossbones symbol.

The vast majority of spiders are very small. However, a small size difference can be significant as you try to identify and study minute and very small spiders. In order that you may immediately grasp the minuteness of some spiders, and the large size of, for instance, tarantulas, average sizes are illustrated below, the spider being measured from the front of the chelicerae to the end of the abdomen, excluding the spinnerets, legs and pedipalps.

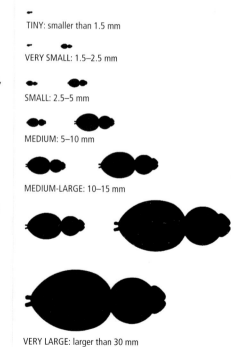

TINY: smaller than 1.5 mm

VERY SMALL: 1.5–2.5 mm

SMALL: 2.5–5 mm

MEDIUM: 5–10 mm

MEDIUM-LARGE: 10–15 mm

VERY LARGE: larger than 30 mm

Millimetres

10   20   30   40   50   60   70

ARANEOMORPHS

Araneomorphs are tiny to very large spiders that belong to the suborder Araneomorphae. They are characterized by having only one pair of book lungs and tracheae (or tracheae only) and diaxial chelicerae. The majority of the web-making and active hunting spiders are araneomorphs.

Orb-web spiders

Ground orb-web weavers

FAMILY: Anapidae

GENERA: *Crozetulus, Dippenaaria, Metanapis, Pseudanapis*

> LIFESTYLE: Sedentary, web-bound,
> free-living
> HABITAT: In forests; in caves
> SIZE: Tiny, 1–1.5 mm
> ACTIVITY: Diurnal/Nocturnal
> DANGER: Harmless
> COLLECTING METHODS: Hand-to-jar;
> tullgren funnel; sifting; pooter

The abdomen of the tiny female anapid is usually covered with two or three scutes. In the male, a large dorsal scute is present on the abdomen, while a ventral scute surrounds the pedicel.

Anapids have a raised carapace. In the male, the patellas of the first pair of legs are very long and have two small apophyses. The spiders breathe through tracheae; no book lungs are present. The anterior median eyes are usually reduced in size or absent. In the female, the pedipalps are also either reduced in size or absent and the legs are spineless.

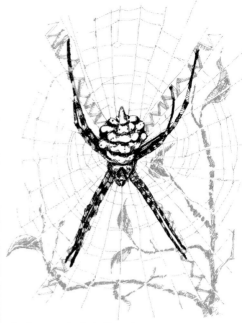

Argiope australis in its web.

Very little is known about the anapids. They are collected mainly from forest litter and caves. *Crozetulus scutatus*, one of four species known in southern Africa, has been collected from the Wynberg caves on Table Mountain.

Anapids were previously placed in the family Leptonetidae.

Orb-web spiders

FAMILY: Araneidae

> DANGER: Harmless
> COLLECTING METHODS: Sweep-
> netting; beating; hand-to-jar; night
> collecting; pooter; tree trap

The araneids are a large family and are diverse in shape, coloration and behaviour. The sexes differ greatly in size and shape, with the mass of the female sometimes being as much as a thousand times that of the male.

Araneids always have three claws on each tarsus, and the third pair of legs is always the shortest.

Orb weavers spin webs as traps in which to ensnare prey, and these are both structurally perfect for their function and things of great beauty.

The family is divided into a range of subfamilies, of which five are known to occur in southern Africa.

GARDEN ORB-WEB SPIDERS

SUBFAMILY: Argiopinae

GENERA: *Argiope, Gea*

**LIFESTYLE: Sedentary, web-bound
HABITAT: In trees; in webs between trees; on bushes and plants or in low base vegetation; on or under grass
SIZE: Medium to large, 6–30 mm; female much larger than male
ACTIVITY: Diurnal**

Female Banded argiope, Argiope trifasciata.

Female Common banded argiope,
Argiope australis.

Gea infuscata *makes its web in grass.*

Most of the *Argiope* species are large, conspicuous spiders, recognized by their silver-grey carapaces, and lobed (in some species), banded, and often yellow, black and silver abdomens. They also have banded, long legs. *Gea* is smaller than most *Argiope* species and has an arched brown carapace. Its abdomen has a distinctive colour pattern, but is not as decorative as that of *Argiope*.

Argiopes spin large webs, usually in tall grass or low bushes, and often in suburban gardens. Their webs have a characteristic zigzag stabilimentum. Argiopes leave their webs in place, and only make running repairs to them if they are damaged.

The female hangs head down in the centre of the web. The front two pairs of legs are held together and forwards, and the back two pairs are held together and backwards, forming a cross. In those species where the stabilimentum itself takes the form of a cross, the legs of the spider rest up against it.

N Larsen

Undescribed male of Argiope aurocincta.

LIFESTYLE: Sedentary, web-bound
HABITAT: In trees; in webs between
trees; on bushes and plants or in low
base vegetation; in forests
SIZE: Medium to medium-large,
5–15 mm; female much larger
than male
ACTIVITY: Diurnal

The abdomen is shiny, hard and dorsally flattened and has a number of lateral and posterior spiny projections. The bright red, orange, yellow, white and black on the abdomen render this spider unmistakable. The tiny male is darker in colour than the female.

N Larsen

Gasteracantha sanguinolenta, *the most commonly found Kite spider.*

All the argiopes react in the same way when prey is ensnared in the web. They approach it, turn, and with a rapid action of the two pairs of back legs, draw out sheets of silken thread to enswathe the prey. Only then do they bite through the wrapping, kill the victim and proceed to feed. This technique of prey capture is not unique to this subfamily: it is common among most of the araneids. If not particularly hungry at the time of prey capture, the spider will carry the prey to the edge of the web and hang it there for future consumption.

The female argiope's egg sac is characteristically camouflaged to blend in with her environment.

KITE SPIDERS

SUBFAMILY: Gasteracanthinae

GENERA: *Gasteracantha, Gastroxya, Hypsacantha, Isoxya, Afracantha*

N Larsen

Kite spider, Gasteracantha falcicornis.

N Larsen

Box kite spider, Isoxya cicatricosa.

In *Gasteracantha*, the abdomen is much wider than it is long, and it usually has long spurs to the side. *Isoxya* has a squarish abdominal plate, with spiny projections at the four corners of the square and on the posterior of the abdomen.

The spinnerets are raised on a slight projection, which is surrounded by a ring of hardened integument.

Female and juvenile Kite spiders are seen hanging in the centre of their vertical (or sometimes inclined at 45 degrees) orb webs. The web is often made between two low *Acacia* trees or in forests, about 2 m above the ground. Sometimes the webs are found high up between tree tops.

Kite spiders take up a position in the centre of the web and wait for prey to fly into the snare threads. The method of prey capture is typical of the other orb-web spiders (see p. 34).

TYPICAL ORB WEAVERS

SUBFAMILY: Araneinae

GENERA: 24 genera including *Araneus, Neoscona, Caerostris, Nemoscolus, Cyclosa, Kilima, Singa, Larinia*

This subfamily includes genera with such distinctive characteristics of looks and behaviour that each genus is treated separately.

Hairy field spiders
GENERA: *Araneus* and *Neoscona*

LIFESTYLE: **Sedentary, web-bound**
HABITAT: **In built-up areas; in trees; in webs between trees; on bushes and plants or in low base vegetation; on or under grass; in forests**
SIZE: **Medium to large, 5–20 mm; female larger than male**
ACTIVITY: **Nocturnal**

Hairy field spider, Neoscona hirta.

Araneus and *Neoscona* are the best known of all the medium to medium-large orb weavers. The abdomen is usually wider than it is long, raised near the anterior and oval or triangularly oval in outline. It often overhangs the carapace. Colour varies from cream to brown to black and from yellow to green, usually with distinct dorsal patterns.

The eyes are set in two rows, with the lateral eyes almost contiguous. The legs are shorter than those of *Argiope* and when the spider is at rest, they fold over or under the body.

The two genera differ in the shape of the thoracic groove, which is usually longitudinal in *Neoscona* and transverse in *Araneus*.

Araneus legonensis *on her silk-covered retreat.*

The males of both genera are smaller and much more angular than the females, and have a less hairy carapace and abdomen. The legs of the males are usually well armed with strong spines, and the size of the pedipalps in mature specimens challenge that of the males of the family Theridiidae (see p. 68).

Hairy field spiders spin their orb webs between two prominent points. The webs vary from tiny and frail to large and robust, but always epitomize the 'perfect orb'. The webs of *Neoscona*, which are often attached to the gutters of houses, can be seen at night; they are removed before daybreak. Most species build their orb web in the late evening and then dismantle it before daybreak by eating the orb section and retaining the support structures for the next night's web.

During the hours of darkness, the spider hangs head down at the hub of the web. During the day, the spider either moves up and into a retreat above the web (after removing the web) or hides under the bark of one of the trees to which the web was attached, sometimes in a retreat.

A characteristic behavioural pattern of Hairy field spiders is their tendency to drop from the hub of the web on a single thread if disturbed, and then either hang suspended there or drop to the substrate. *Araneus* must surely be the spider that dropped down beside Little Miss Muffet.

Garbage line spiders
GENUS: *Cyclosa*

> **LIFESTYLE: Sedentary, web-bound**
> **HABITAT: In webs between trees;**
> **on bushes and plants or in low base**
> **vegetation; on or under grass;**
> **in forests**
> **SIZE: Small to medium-large, 4–11 mm**
> **ACTIVITY: Diurnal**

Garbage line spider, Cyclosa *sp.*

In the female *Cyclosa*, the abdomen has a distinct caudal tubercle protruding past the spinnerets, which varies in size and becomes more prominent with age. It is absent in males. The abdomen is usually silver or grey. The first pair of legs is longer than the rest.

The eyes are situated on a prominent tubercle at the front of a usually shiny, brownish carapace.

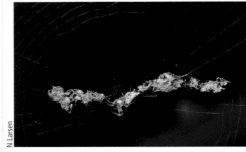

Cyclosa *sp hidden in its garbage line.*

The Garbage line spider builds its web between grasses and bushes. The web may be distinguished from those of other orb weavers by its stabilimentum stretched across the centre of a meshed hub (distinct from the zigzag stabilimentum of *Argiope*, for example). The stabilimentum may be vertically or horizontally positioned, and is made up of prey remains, debris, cast exoskeletons of the spider and other bits and pieces, all woven in and attached to the web with thick white silk.

The spider positions itself in the centre of the 'garbage line' with its legs stretched forwards and backwards, or hunched up. In this way, the spider is completely camouflaged. Unlike the cribellate spider *Uloborus* (see p. 49), which attempts to escape when disturbed, *Cyclosa* doggedly clings to the stabilimentum, even under extreme provocation.

Bark spiders

GENUS: *Caerostris*

> **LIFESTYLE: Sedentary, web-bound**
> **HABITAT: In trees; in webs between trees; on or under bark**
> **SIZE: Medium to large, 8–21 mm**
> **ACTIVITY: Nocturnal**

Anterior view of the common Bark spider, Caerostris sexcuspidata.

Posterior view showing animal face, Caerostris sexcuspidata.

Bark spider, Caerostris corticosa, *with egg sac.*

Bark spiders have horny or leathery protuberances on the abdomen, which resemble the bark or thorns of trees. Their legs are covered with fine hair and, when at rest, fold in around the spider. The abdomen overhangs the carapace. The eight small eyes are on a tubercle on the front of the carapace. *Caerostris* can easily be identified by the four tiny, blunt, horn-like projections on the carapace and the animal face on the abdomen when viewed from the rear.

At dusk – after establishing a long and sturdy bridge line – Bark spiders construct a very large orb web, which can span 1–1.5 m in diameter. The bridge line may measure up to 2 m between attachment points. At dawn the spider dismantles the web, leaving only the bridge line, and 'disappears' onto the nearest tree. *Caerostris sexcuspidata* is partly diurnal in forested areas.

Stone nest spiders
GENUS: *Nemoscolus*

LIFESTYLE: **Sedentary, web-bound**
HABITAT: **On rocks or in crevices of rocks; on bushes and plants or in low base vegetation; on or under grass**
SIZE: **Medium, 6–10 mm**
ACTIVITY: **Diurnal**

Stone nest spider web and retreat of Nemoscolus.

Nemoscolus has an elliptical abdomen, the dorsal aspect of which has distinct white markings. In some species the abdomen extends past the spinnerets.

Nemoscolus constructs orb webs up to 20 cm in diameter, most often horizontally. The webs are found in rocky grasslands, especially near rocky outcrops and low-hanging trees. A retreat is always constructed, varying in shape between species from an inverted cone to a spiral-like cornucopia. This shelter is constructed of tough silken threads, into which are woven grains of sand, vegetable debris, and even shells of consumed prey. The retreat is secured above the hub of the web with tough silken threads, which pull the centre of the web upwards into a cone shape. This retreat is also used for the egg sac and as an early nursery for the spiderlings.

Scorpion-tailed spiders
GENUS: *Arachnura*

LIFESTYLE: **Sedentary, web-bound**
HABITAT: **On bushes and plants or in low base vegetation; in forests**
SIZE: **Medium, 15 mm**
ACTIVITY: **Diurnal/Nocturnal**

Arachnura scorpionoides *constructing her egg sac.*

Scorpion-tailed spider, Arachnura scorpionoides, *with a captured fly.*

Undescribed Arachnura *species.*

These spiders are rare in southern Africa, with *Arachnura scorpionoides* being the only described species. Two further species have been collected. The generic name is derived from the Greek words *arachne* (spider) and *ura* (tail). The abdomen of *Arachnura* has two anterior conical projections. Posteriorly the abdomen tapers past the spinnerets and ends in two projections. The tail is prehensile and can be extended and curled in various directions (similar to a scorpion's tail). The female is light brown, straw colour or yellow. The small male lacks a tail and is rarely seen.

The small orb webs of these spiders are constructed among vegetation, usually with a section missing in the top of the web. The egg sac is built in the hub of the web, whereafter the web is rebuilt. It eventually houses a string of six egg cases, below which the spider hangs.

Grass orb-web spiders
GENUS: *Larinia*

LIFESTYLE: Sedentary, web-bound
HABITAT: On or under grass
SIZE: Small to medium, 4–10 mm
ACTIVITY: Nocturnal

In *Larinia*, the abdomen is more than twice as long as it is wide, and overlaps the cephalothorax. These spiders are yellowish-brown with dark longitudinal stripes along the dorsal aspect of the abdomen. On their webs, they characteristically hold the two front pairs of legs together and forwards, and the two pairs of back legs together and backwards.

Grass orb-web spider, Larinia bifida.

In the early morning the webs can be seen hanging in among the grass. When not in the web, *Larinia* may rest on grass stems, like some members of the families Philodromidae and Thomisidae.

TROPICAL TENT-WEB SPIDERS
SUBFAMILY: Cyrtophorinae

GENUS: *Cyrtophora*

LIFESTYLE: Sedentary, web-bound
HABITAT: In built-up areas; in trees;
on bushes and plants or in low base
vegetation; near fresh water
SIZE: Medium to medium-large,
8–15 mm
ACTIVITY: Diurnal/Nocturnal

The abdomen of *Cyrtophora* is longer than it is wide, and raised, with distinct, blunt tubercles. Colour varies from cream to black, with white markings seen on all species. Only one species, *Cyrtophora citricola*, has been identified in southern Africa.

The distinctive web is a globe of crisscrossed, tangled threads, commonly

N Larsen

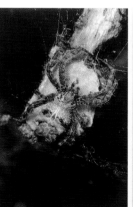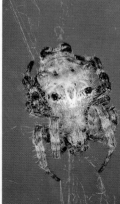

Tropical tent-web spiders, Cyrtophora citricola, on egg sac (left), and on web (right).

found in the middle of low base vegetation or in aloes and cacti, but also in and around suburban gardens. In the centre of the globe lies a horizontal or near-horizontal fine orb web, sometimes pulled up slightly at the hub to form a tent-like sheet.

The spider hangs beneath the web while awaiting prey. The tangled threads and foundation lines of the web act as knockdown threads; prey flying into them falls onto the horizontal orb web. The spider then moves to the prey and, through the web, bites and subdues it.

Rather like in the web of *Cyclosa*, there may be what looks like prey remains dotted around the hub. These are usually disguised egg sacs. *Cyrtophora* hangs perfectly camouflaged below these egg sacs when at rest. If the spider is disturbed, it drops down into the undergrowth, immediately changing its colour to a shade of black to match its new surroundings.

SUBFAMILY: Cyrtarachninae

Hedgehog spiders
GENUS: *Pycnacantha*

> LIFESTYLE: Sedentary
> HABITAT: On bushes and plants or in low base vegetation; on or under grass
> SIZE: Medium-large, 8–15 mm
> ACTIVITY: Nocturnal

The abdomen of the hedgehog spider is covered with numerous sharp, spine-like protuberances, giving it the appearance of a hedgehog. The spines of juvenile spiders are shorter than those of the adults. It lives in grass; when at rest, with its legs pulled back, it resembles a grass seed. *Pycnacantha* hunts among the grass and sometimes in woody bush without a web

Hedgehog spider, Pycnacantha tribulus.

Observations made of a captive specimen reveal that the egg sac is cone-shaped, with the apex hanging downwards from the web. The egg sac is constructed of light yellow silk.

Ladybird spiders
GENUS: *Paraplectana*

> LIFESTYLE: Sedentary, web-bound
> HABITAT: On bushes and plants or in low base vegetation; on or under grass
> SIZE: Small to medium, 3–8 mm
> ACTIVITY: Diurnal

The abdomen of this orb-web spider is round and decorated with black spots or markings on a bright yellow or red background. Not commonly seen but very distinctive, it is easy to recognize if found. These spiders appear to specialize in capturing moths with the use of an orb web.

L Oates

Ladybird spider, Paraplectana thorntoni.

African bolas spiders
GENUS: *Cladomelea*

LIFESTYLE: Free-running, plant-living
HABITAT: On bushes and plants
or in low base vegetation; on or
under grass
SIZE: Medium to medium-large,
8–15 mm
ACTIVITY: Nocturnal

Cladomelea is related to the bolas spiders of America and Australia. It is one of the numerous exceptions to the rule in that it does not make an orb web. (Morphologically, however, it is

similar to other orb-web spiders and is therefore classified as such.) Rather, it constructs a nest – used as a retreat by day – by pulling grass or leaves together with a binding of silken threads. Within this framework, egg sacs are constructed and attached.

At nightfall the spider moves to an upper portion of the nest and hangs from a bridge line. It produces a sticky droplet from its spinnerets, attaches it to a thread long enough to suspend the droplet a few centimetres above the ground, and swings it around. The thread is held by the third leg (or legs) and not by the front legs as is the case with other bolas spiders. A pheromone in the droplet attracts male moths into the path of the swinging ball. Once the prey is captured, the spider reels in the thread. Several of these droplets and lines may be constructed during one night.

Bird-dropping spiders
GENERA: *Aethriscus, Cyrtarachne*

LIFESTYLE: Sedentary, plant-living
HABITAT: On flowers or leaves
SIZE: Medium-large, 10–15 mm
ACTIVITY: Diurnal

The Bird-dropping spider has a smooth, glistening abdomen; as it rests on a leaf it resembles the wet excrement of a bird. It has been suggested that this mimicry is a defence mechanism to prevent the spider being preyed

J Leroy

African bolas spider, Cladomelea akermani, *swinging a sticky droplet from a thread.*

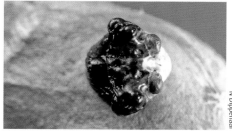

N Dippenaar

Bird-dropping spider, Aethriscus olivaceus.

S Adams

Bird-dropping spider, Cyrtarachne *sp.*

The large, colourful Golden orb-web spider's elongated, cylindrical abdomen (marked in contrasting colours of black and yellow or white and yellow) and extremely long legs (which give it a delicate look) make it easily recognizable. On the carapace, silver hairs cover most of the dark brown to black undertone. Two of the

on by foraging birds and other predators. However, other writers suggest that certain butterflies and several types of fly are attracted to bird droppings for the salts they contain. The mimicry therefore serves two purposes: attracting prey and repelling predators.

Like the bolas spider, *Aethriscus* does not make a web snare, but hangs under a leaf in a reduced web and preys on moths. *Cyrtarachne* constructs a spanning web that catches prey.

Golden orb-web spiders

FAMILY: Nephilidae

GENERA: *Nephila* (Golden orb-web spiders), *Nephilengys* (Hermit spiders), *Clitaetra*

> LIFESTYLE: Sedentary, web-bound
> HABITAT: In trees; in webs between trees; on bushes and plants or in low base vegetation; in forests
> SIZE: Medium to very large; *Nephila* 25–30 mm, *Nephilengys* 10–28 mm, *Clitaetra* 7–10 mm; female much larger than small male
> ACTIVITY: Diurnal
> DANGER: Harmless
> COLLECTING METHOD: Hand-to-jar

N Larsen

Female Black-legged nephila, Nephila fenestrata, *on her egg sac.*

C Haddad

Female Banded-legged nephila, Nephila senegalensis, *on her web.*

M Kuntner
M Kuntner
M Kuntner

Female Red-legged nephila, Nephila inaurata.

Clitaetra irenae female in her web against the bark of a tree.

Nephilengys cruentata is known as the Hermit spider.

three species in the region, namely *Nephila senegalensis* and *Nephila fenestrata*, have tufts of coarse hair on the tibiae and femora of the first, second and fourth pairs of legs, and *N. senegalensis* has clear yellow bands on its legs. The female *Nephila* is many times larger than the male, her body mass being as much as a thousand times more than his.

Nephilengys is slightly smaller in size than *Nephila*, and its distribution is limited to the northeastern regions of southern Africa. Most species are distinctive in having a bright yellow to orange-red sternum and their legs, like those of *N. senegalensis*, are banded.

The Golden orb-web spider hangs head down in the hub of its web, in which the debris of old prey is sometimes strung out in a line from the top to the bottom of the web to resemble a stabilimentum. Juveniles, both male and female, spin a complete orb, but only female adults spin webs of strong, thick, golden silk. The adult spider does not spin a complete web, leaving out the 'top section' of the orb, but because of all the attending threads it is difficult to notice that a section is missing. The whole construction is linked to branches and twigs with irregular, tough strands, which also serve as knockdown lines. Kleptoparasites such as *Argyrodes* (see p. 70) are often found in the orb webs of *Nephila*.

Nephilengys is known as the Hermit spider, as it makes a retreat to the side of its web. Its silk is white and its web, like that of *Nephila*, is not a full orb. In place of the missing portion, there is often a funnel-like retreat, which may be seen in the forks of trees, in rock crevices and on walls. The spider only emerges from the retreat to catch prey.

Clitaetra irenae, the only southern African species, occurs in coastal forest in northern KwaZulu-Natal. It constructs a ladder-shaped orb web against smooth-barked trees.

Long- and Thick-jawed spiders, Silver marsh spiders and Cave orb spiders

FAMILY: Tetragnathidae

GENERA: *Tetragnatha* (Long-jawed water spiders), *Pachygnatha* (Thick-jawed spiders), *Leucauge* (Silver marsh spiders), *Meta* (Cave orb spiders), *Diphya*

> LIFESTYLE: Sedentary, web-bound; free-running, ground-living
> HABITAT: In webbing or scrapes under stones; on bushes and plants or in low base vegetation; on or under grass; in and under leaf litter and rotting logs; near fresh water
> SIZE: Very small to large, 2–23 mm; *Tetragnatha* medium to medium-large, 6–15 mm (excluding chelicerae; leg span >30 mm); *Pachygnatha* medium to medium-large, 6–12 mm; *Leucauge* medium to medium-large, 7–15 mm; *Meta* medium to medium-large, 6–13 mm; female slightly larger than male
> ACTIVITY: Nocturnal; *Tetragnatha* and *Leucauge* diurnal
> DANGER: Harmless
> COLLECTING METHODS: Sweep-netting; beating; hand-to-jar

N Larsen

Long-jawed water spider, Tetragnatha boydi.

Tetragnatha *chelicerae and carapace.*

The five genera in this family differ greatly in outward characteristics. *Tetragnatha* is distinctive in shape and colour. It has a long and slender body, with well-developed, elongated chelicerae and long legs. It is light yellow to reddish-brown or grey, with silver and gold markings on the abdomen. The abdomen is usually broad at the base, tapering towards the spinnerets. The chelicerae are a diagnostic feature.

N Larsen

Festive silver marsh spider, Leucauge festiva.

Pachygnatha has a much more globose abdomen, looking more like a large theridiid (see p. 68) than like its near relatives. Its chelicerae are more robust and thickened, and its legs not quite as delicate and long as those of *Tetragnatha*. Its carapace is usually yellow, with an obscure border and a median band.

Leucauge, the Silver marsh or Orchard spider, is a brightly coloured spider resembling a miniature nephilid. Its abdomen is silver patterned with green, yellow and red markings, and is longer than it is wide. *Leucauge* may be distinguished from *Meta* by its colourful abdomen and the presence of a fringe of curled hairs on the femora of its fourth pair of legs.

Sexual dimorphism is not marked, the male being similar to the female. The male *Leucauge* does, however, have a more slender body and noticeably swollen palps.

Meta looks rather like a large theridiid: its abdomen is globose with brownish-yellow markings, and its legs have obvious setae. Being an inhabitant of dark, damp places, *Meta* is seldom disturbed. As a result, its web is often immaculate. A large, white, translucent egg sac is often seen hanging by a thread above the web.

Tetragnatha, the Long-jawed water spider, construct a typical wagon-wheel web. The web is constructed near or above a stream and is usually set at a slight angle or horizontally. Unique to this orb web is the absence of a central hub. On the web, the spider hangs upside-down with its first and second pairs of legs stretched forward. Unlike many of the other orb-web spiders, tetragnathids do not stay permanently on the web and may be found roaming freely or resting on grass stems or twigs. At rest, six of the long spindly legs are stretched out (the first and second pairs to the front and the fourth to the back), while the shorter third pair of legs embraces the twig. The male's chelicerae are longer than those of the female and have a spur protruding from the inner frontal area. The spur is used to hold the female's jaws safely apart while mating.

Spiders from the genus *Pachygnatha* are hunters. The adults do not build a web, but the young are known to build small orb webs. Not much is known about their behaviour other than that they are found under stones, especially in the vicinity of damp places, and under rotting logs and moist leaf litter.

The webs of the *Meta* are small and are built mostly horizontally. *Meta* makes its

A new species of Meta *from Table Mountain National Park.*

N Larsen

web among boulders and tree trunks near streams, especially in mountainous terrain, and also in the entrances of caves and grottos. The web has the typical open hub of the long-jawed spiders.

Leucauge spins a large, inclined web in grass and reeds, nearly always close to water. Unlike the web of *Meta*, this web does have a central hub. The spider rests at the hub with its head down, below the web. An open space is clearly visible between the hub and the viscid catch zone of the outer web. Some species of *Leucauge* build an accompanying barrier web under the orb, in which the spider rests. The size of the web is very large in relation to the size of the spider.

Ray spiders

FAMILY: Theridiosomatidae

GENERA: *Baalzebub, Wendilgarda*

LIFESTYLE: Sedentary, web-bound
HABITAT: In trees; on bushes and plants or in low base vegetation; in forests
SIZE: Tiny to small, 0.5–3 mm
ACTIVITY: Nocturnal
DANGER: Harmless
COLLECTING METHODS: Hand-to-jar

Ray spider in its web.

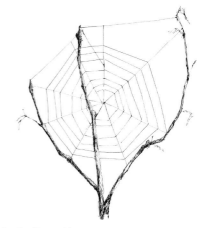

Web of a Ray spider.

The theridiosomatids are very small spiders. They can be identified by the presence of pits on the front margin of the sternum in both sexes. In many ways (as their name suggests) they resemble small theridiids (see p. 68). They have eight eyes in two rows, the carapace is pear-shaped, and the chelicerae are robust. Their legs appear heavy for such small spiders. The abdomen is smoothly ovoid or has variously placed tubercles. The spider is usually uniform in colour, or has transverse silvery or white bands. When in their small webs with their legs pulled up alongside the body, these spiders look like a small seed caught up in a spider's web.

Theridiosomatids live almost exclusively in wet or humid areas, such as forests. Their webs are diverse, but they always spin a complete orb. Indeed, their webs are a distinguishing feature. For many years, they were mistakenly classified as a subfamily of orb-web spiders.

Wendilgarda constructs a tension line more or less at right angles to the plane of the web, which the spider reels in to distort the orb into a conical form. When the spider releases the tension line, the web springs back to ensnare the prey.

Dwarf orb weavers

FAMILY: Symphytognathidae

GENERA: *Symphytognatha, Patu*

> **LIFESTYLE: Sedentary, web-bound;**
> **free-running, ground-living**
> **HABITAT: In and under leaf litter**
> **and rotting logs; in forests**
> **SIZE: Tiny to very small, <2 mm**
> **ACTIVITY: Diurnal/Nocturnal**
> **DANGER: Harmless**
> **COLLECTING METHODS: Hand-to-jar;**
> **pitfall trap; tullgren funnel; sifting;**
> **pooter**

Dwarf orb-weaver measures less than 2 mm.

As New Zealand author Forster says, 'If you can think small enough, they are easy to find!' The chelicerae of these tiny, yellow-brown spiders are fused at the base. The pedipalp of the female is absent or reduced to one segment. Dwarf orb weavers have four or six eyes (*Symphytognatha* has six), which are arranged in diads or triads on a pronounced carapace. Book lungs are absent.

Little is known about these spiders in southern Africa, and they are rarely found. Typically cryptozoic, they inhabit high-humidity areas, such as forest floors and under damp leaf litter. Although they never measure more than 2 mm in length, it is amazing to see their small orb webs stretched across the mossy ground cover and on the moist, moss-covered lower trunks of trees in damp forest areas. Although some construct orb webs, others have lost the ability to be web-bound.

Cribellate-web spiders

Hackled orb-web spiders

FAMILY: Uloboridae

GENERA: *Miagrammopes, Uloborus, Hyptiotes, Philoponella*

This family is unique in being the only family of spiders that does not possess venom glands. As cribellate spiders, they build different kinds of webs, varying from single-line webs to orb webs.

Single-line web spiders

GENUS: *Miagrammopes*

> **LIFESTYLE: Sedentary, web-bound**
> **HABITAT: On bushes and plants or in**
> **low base vegetation**
> **SIZE: Small to medium, 3–10 mm**
> **ACTIVITY: Nocturnal**
> **DANGER: Harmless**
> **COLLECTING METHODS: Beating;**
> **hand-to-jar; night collecting**

Also known as the Tropical stick spider, *Miagrammopes* is small, with a long, narrow carapace and a cylindrical abdomen, which is truncated above the spinnerets or extends over it. The anterior eye row is absent, leaving only four eyes in the posterior eye row. The eyes are recurved and widely spaced over the carapace.

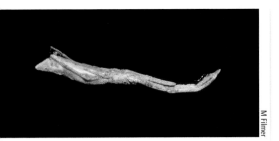

M Filmer

Single-line web spider, Miagrammopes.

Miagrammopes is unique among Uloboridae in spinning a single-line web. The foundation is usually a horizontal strand between two branches or twigs. The length of the strand varies from one to three metres. Only the section in the middle is covered with cribellate silk: this is the catch web. Hanging below the web, the spider grips the branch or a few threads attached to the branch with its hind legs. With its front legs, it holds the foundation thread under tension.

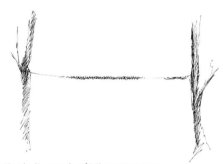

Single-line web of Miagrammopes.

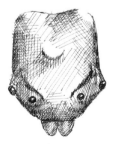

Carapace of Miagrammopes *showing eye pattern.*

The different species use slightly different techniques to catch prey, but in general, it involves a jerking and sudden sagging of the catch web as the prey touches it. As the prey is ensnared, the spider rushes forwards along the line to devour it. *Miagrammopes* makes its web during the night, resting close to the supporting branch during the day.

Hackled orb-web spiders
GENUS: *Uloborus*

LIFESTYLE: Sedentary, web-bound
HABITAT: In built-up areas; in trees;
on bushes and trees or in low base
vegetation
SIZE: Medium, 5–8 mm
ACTIVITY: Nocturnal
DANGER: Harmless
COLLECTING METHODS: Sweep-netting; beating; hand-to-jar

Uloborus is a smallish spider with a sedentary nature. It is characterized by its long front legs held apart, rather humped abdomen and almost horizontal orb web. The female *Uloborus plumipes* (Feather-legged spider), which is frequently found in and around houses, has a brush of coarse, long hairs on the tibiae of the first pair of legs. The eyes of *Uloborus* are arranged in two separated, curved rows.

The orb webs of *Uloborus* are horizontal or obliquely inclined. The hub of the web is often meshed or strengthened with a stabilimentum. The spider sits in the centre of the web, legs stretched out along the strands of the stabilimentum. This renders the spider difficult to see, unless it is disturbed. *Uloborus* builds its web in low bushes, between objects near the ground and often in large cacti and succulents; it is also common in forests and in and around outbuildings.

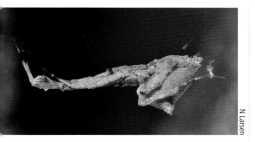

Introduced Feather-legged spider,
Uloborus plumipes.

Web of a Hackled orb-web spider, Uloborus.

Triangle-web spiders

GENUS: *Hyptiotes*

> LIFESTYLE: Sedentary, web-bound
> HABITAT: On bushes and plants or
> in low base vegetation
> SIZE: Small to medium, 4–8 mm
> ACTIVITY: Diurnal/Nocturnal
> DANGER: Harmless
> COLLECTING METHODS: Sweep-
> netting; beating; hand-to-jar

Not very common and rather inconspicuous because of its light-brown ground colour, *Hyptiotes* is generally recognized in the field only by its web. It normally rests close to a branch, using its body as a bridge between the branch and its triangle web. At rest, the spider resembles a dried-up bud and as a result, is often overlooked.

The abdomen is short, oval, humped and rather drab in colour. The legs are shorter and stouter than those of other Uloboridae. The eyes are a diagnostic feature of this genus. The posterior row is placed well back on the carapace and is wider than the anterior row.

At first glance, the web looks like a fragment of a complete orb web. It consists of only four radial lines attached to a holding thread and supporting a variable number of catch threads made of cribellate silk. Pulling the holding thread tight but allowing some loose line to hang below, the spider awaits its prey. When an insect is caught in the web, the spider releases the line, causing a 'spring action' that further ensnares the prey.

So far, only one species has been identified in South Africa, namely *Hyptiotes akermani*, which was collected in KwaZulu-Natal.

Triangle-web spider, Hyptiotes, *holding its web.*

Mesh-web spiders

FAMILY: Amaurobiidae

GENERA: *Chresiona* (ecribellate),
Macrobunus, Obatala, Pseudauximus

> LIFESTYLE: Sedentary, ground-living
> HABITAT: In webbing, under stones;
> in and under leaf litter and rotting
> logs; in forests
> SIZE: Small to large, 3–16 mm
> ACTIVITY: Nocturnal
> DANGER: Harmless
> COLLECTING METHODS: Hand-to-jar;
> night collecting; pitfall trap; sifting;
> rock turning

N Larsen

Mesh-web spider, Chresiona, *on a* Roridula dentata *plant.*

A family of rather drab, ground-living spiders. One species, which is not so drab, lives on the glandular *Roridula dentata*. This plant is unable to absorb insects caught on its sticky tentacles, and the spider is able to obtain an easy meal. Amaurobiidae are three-clawed, cribellate spiders, with one genus being ecribellate. Afrotropical genera belong to the subfamily Macrobuninae. The subfamily Phyxelidinae has been elevated to family status.

Forest hackled mesh-weavers

FAMILY: Phyxelididae

GENERA: *Lamaika, Malaika, Matundua, Namaquarachne, Pongolania, Xevioso, Phyxelida, Themacrys, Vidole*

> LIFESTYLE: Sedentary, ground-living
> HABITAT: In webbing, under stones; on rocks or in crevices of rocks; in and under leaf litter and rotting logs; in forests; in caves
> SIZE: Small to large, 3–16 mm
> ACTIVITY: Nocturnal
> DANGER: Harmless
> COLLECTING METHODS: Hand-to-jar; night collecting; pitfall trap; sifting; rock turning

Phyxelididae was previously a subfamily of Amaurobiidae. Similar to Amaurobiidae, the spiders in this family are drab and live on the ground. They are the most common cribellate spiders in southern Africa. All genera have a distinctly divided cribellum.

The carapace is longer than it is wide, and the eyes (light in colour in most species) are arranged in two rows. The abdomen is oval, with ill-defined dorsal patterns. The legs (especially those of the males) are fairly long. The metatarsi of the males' first pair of legs are strongly modified.

The phyxelidids prefer cool, damp places, and are typical representatives of southern African cryptozoic fauna. However, certain genera (for example, *Vidole*) are found in the drier parts of the country, while some genera (such as *Malaika, Phyxelida* and *Themacrys*)

Vidole capensis, *the Fynbos hackled mesh-weaver.*

Malaika longipes, *the Forest hackled mesh-weaver.*

Malaika longipes, the Forest hackled mesh-weaver in its web.

Metatarsus of the family Phyxelididae.

are found in caves. Three species have been identified in open thorn bush and savanna.

Forest hackled mesh-weavers construct easily recognizable, irregular, tangled webs, which are found under stones, in rock crevices or trees and under rotten logs on the forest floor. The webs of some species, made of bluish cribellate silk, have a typical doily-like appearance.

Velvet spiders

FAMILY: Eresidae

GENERA: *Dresserus, Gandanameno, Paradonea, Penestomus, Stegodyphus, Seothyra*

> LIFESTYLE: Sedentary, web-bound; free-running, ground-living; sedentary, ground-living; sedentary, plant-living
> ACTIVITY: Diurnal/Nocturnal

The eresids are corpulent spiders. The carapace is bluntly rounded in front, and the spiders usually have thick, short legs. The median eyes are set close to each other, while both pairs of lateral eyes are set far apart from the median eyes. There is usually sexual dimorphism, with the males smaller and different in colour. Penestomus has been elevated to 70th family, Penestomidae.

Horned velvet spiders and Tree velvet spiders

GENERA: *Dresserus, Gandanameno*

> HABITAT: *Dresserus* in webbing or scrapes under stones; *Gandanameno* on or under bark
> SIZE: Small to large, 3–20 mm; female usually larger than male
> DANGER: Harmless
> COLLECTING METHODS: *Dresserus* hand-to-jar, pitfall trap, rock turning; *Gandanameno* hand-to-jar

Dresserus and *Gandanameno* are black or dark brown to reddish-brown. The spiders are covered in fine hairs, which gives them a velvety appearance. The cephalic area in both males and females is weakly

N Larsen

Female Tree velvet spider, Gandanameno
fumosa, *showing her velvety carapace.*

raised, with the fovea present as a circular
pit. *Dresserus* has a tri- or quadripartite
cribellum, and the males have horn-like
tubercles on the edge of the carapace.
Gandanameno has a bipartite cribellum.

Species of *Dresserus* are usually found
under stones, where they build messy,
bluish-white, shroud-like retreats of loosely
woven silk embedded with grains of sand.
The retreat hangs like a pendulous sac when
the stone is lifted. These spiders are loath

to emerge from their webs and have to be
gently prized out. Sluggish and generally not
aggressive, they are easy to capture.

Spiders of the genus *Gandanameno* are
usually found under the loose bark or in the
crevices and old knotholes of trees. They build
funnel-like webs in crevices. The entrance
to the web shelters under a tarpaulin-like,
flat and solid web and is anchored to the
substrate with scalloped, tough, silken
threads. Well-established females in old trees
or trees with loosened bark may present
a veritable maze of webbing and tunnels,
making them very difficult to find and collect.

Both *Dresserus* and *Gandanameno* can be
found throughout southern Africa.

Decorated velvet spiders
GENUS: *Paradonea*

**HABITAT: In webbing, scrapes
or free-running, under stones;
in semi-arid desert
SIZE: Medium-large to large, 12–30 mm;
female usually larger than male
DANGER: Harmless
COLLECTING METHODS: Hand-to-jar;
pitfall trap; rock turning**

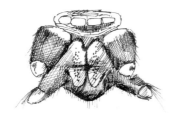

The quadripartite cribellum of Dresserus.

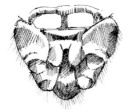

The bipartite cribellum of Gandanameno.

Dorsal view of Paradonea, *the Decorated
velvet spider.*

Decorated velvet spiders are large, although the males are smaller than the females. *Paradonea* is black with white markings or brown to black with white spots on the abdomen. The carapace is raised and slopes strongly to the rear. The abdomen is oval to round in shape. In some species, the anterior lateral eyes are set on prominent tubercles.

Little is known about the behaviour of *Paradonea*. It is found in Namibia, Little Namaqualand, parts of the Western Cape (including Worcester), the North West province (Marico) and Pretoria.

Community nest spiders
GENUS: *Stegodyphus*

> **HABITAT: In trees; in webs between trees; on bushes and plants or in low base vegetation**
> **SIZE: Small to large, 3.5–23 mm; female usually larger than male**
> **DANGER: Harmless**
> **COLLECTING METHODS: Beating; hand-to-jar**

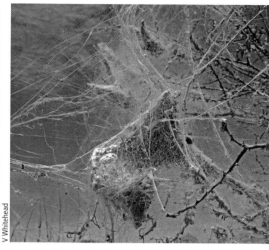

V Whitehead

Stegodyphus dumicola *web.*

N Larsen

Community nest spiders, Stegodyphus dumicola, *with* Philanthus *wasp.*

The common name for this genus is misleading, as only *Stegodyphus dumicola* and *Stegodyphus mimosarum* are social species – four other species live solitary lives. It is these social species that are most easily noticed.

Community nest spiders are greyish-brown, usually with patterns on the abdomen. The males are smaller and more brightly coloured than the females. The carapace is slightly raised and distinctively clothed in white hairs. In *Stegodyphus dumicola*, a triangular pattern of white hairs is present between the eyes.

Stegodyphus is most often noticed because of the large and untidy nest it constructs in trees, usually *Acacia*. A large number of females, males and juveniles live together in one nest. They use cribellate silk to spin the nest, which consists of a retreat of numerous tunnels and chambers, and a web, which is used to catch prey. The catch webs, set out at various angles to the retreat, are attached to nearby branches. Prey that lands on a catch web is killed by a party of spiders and dragged into or close to the retreat. The community then gathers for the feast.

A genus belonging to the family Dictynidae, *Archaeodictyna* (see p. 55), may sometimes be found living in harmony with the eresids in their community webs.

Stegodyphus is found throughout southern Africa. In areas like the Free State where trees are scarce, they build their nests on fences.

Buckspoor spiders

GENUS: *Seothyra*

> **HABITAT: On or under sand; in burrows; in semi-arid desert**
> **SIZE: Medium to medium-large, 5–14.5 mm; female usually larger than male**
> **DANGER: Little is known about their venom, but according to people from Namibia, the Bushmen used the spider's venom on their arrowheads to kill prey**
> **COLLECTING METHODS: Pitfall traps (males); hand-to-jar; digging (females and juveniles)**

Seothyra is reddish-brown to fawn, with some species having markings on the abdomen. Distinctive of this genus are the minute posterior and median spinnerets, which are scarcely half the length of the anterior ones. These spiders are smaller than the other eresids, and distinct sexual dimorphism exists in that the males (*Camponotus* ant and mutillid wasp mimics) differ completely from the females in size, shape, colour and behaviour.

The female *Seothyra* lives below the ground. It digs a tubular retreat, covering it with a two- or four-lobed carpet of silk and sand that resembles an animal spoor. This 'spoor' is most easily detected in the early morning or late afternoon when the sun throws long shadows on the ground. Many such nests may be found in one area.

The female spider positions herself underneath the web, grabbing from underneath any prey walking over the silk carpet. The *Seothyra* diurnal male runs

E de Kock

Female Fasciated buckspoor spider, Seothyra fasciata.

J Henschel

The Henschel's buckspoor spider is a Camponotus ant mimic.

B Vivier

Typical Buckspoor spider web.

around actively on the surface capturing prey, mimicking the ants that live in the vicinity.

To date, Buckspoor spiders have only been found in southern Africa. They are common in the more arid regions of Namibia, the Northern and Western Cape and Limpopo.

Crevice spiders

FAMILY: Filistatidae

GENUS: *Afrofilistata*

> LIFESTYLE: Sedentary, ground-living
> HABITAT: In webbing under stones; on rocks or in crevices of rocks
> SIZE: Small to medium-large, 3–15 mm
> ACTIVITY: Nocturnal
> DANGER: Harmless
> COLLECTING METHODS: Hand-to-jar; rock turning

Afrofilistata is a light yellow to brown cribellate spider without any distinctive markings. It is similar in general appearance to the amaurobiids (see p. 49). The carapace does, however, have a distinctive shape. The eight eyes are tightly clustered in the centre front of the carapace on a small tubercle. *Afrofilistata* has long legs (especially males), the first pair being the longest. A diagnostic feature is that the labium is fused to the sternum. The cribellum is difficult to see and can easily be missed. The spinnerets are more ventral than terminal.

Crevice spiders are sedentary. They live their lives in rather untidy cribellate webs in the natural crevices of rocks and under rocks. The tubular webs are easy to spot, often being built up and over the upper surface of the rock. Owing to its sticky nature, the web is usually encrusted with dust.

Crevice spiders are found in Namibia and the Northern Cape.

Plant mesh-web spiders

FAMILY: Dictynidae

GENERA: *Anaxibia, Archaeodictyna, Dictyna, Shango, Mashimo, Nigma*

> LIFESTYLE: Sedentary, web-bound
> HABITAT: In trees; on bushes and plants or in low base vegetation; in forests
> SIZE: Small to medium, 3–5 mm
> ACTIVITY: Diurnal/Nocturnal
> DANGER: Harmless
> COLLECTING METHODS: Sweep-netting; beating; hand-to-jar; pooter

The dictynids are small spiders. They have a wide cribellum and a uniserate calamistrum, but are generally recognized only by their unique webs. The abdomen may slightly overlap the carapace and is usually decorated with light and dark patterns. The carapace is distinctly high and usually covered in white hairs. The eyes are arranged in two straight rows and are more or less the same size. The anterior median eyes are dark; the other six eyes appear pearly white. The chelicerae are typically long and indented.

N Larsen

Plant mesh-web spider, Dictynidae, *with prey.*

Web of Dictynidae.

Most Plant mesh-web spiders seem to be solitary. They construct small, irregular webs as traps to catch prey. The webs are often anchored at the terminal points of branches and dried twigs, and a few are found on walls. A framework is constructed with simple dry lines, then crisscrossed with cribellate silk to form a symmetrical sheet or lattice. Within the web, the female builds a small retreat for herself, and in summer the male may sometimes be found there with her.

The dictynids are common throughout southern Africa.

Net-casting spiders

FAMILY: Deinopidae

GENERA: *Deinopis, Menneus, Avellopsis*

LIFESTYLE: Free-running, plant-living
ACTIVITY: Nocturnal
DANGER: Harmless

The spiders in this family are stick-like in appearance, and they have a remarkable and unique method of capturing prey. Deinopidae spiders' most distinctive characteristics are the abdomen's modification with one or two humps (with some exceptions); the eye pattern (see illustration of *Deinopis*); the long legs; and the method of prey capture.

Ogre-faced spiders
GENUS: *Deinopis*

HABITAT: In trees; on bushes and plants or in low base vegetation; in forests
SIZE: Medium-large to large, 12–20 mm; female slightly larger than male
COLLECTING METHODS: Beating; hand-to-jar; night collecting

J Leroy

Web of Dictynidae.

The female Ogre-faced spider is uniformly blackish-brown and coated with whitish-yellow hairs. In the male, the carapace and abdomen are dark olive-brown with silver-white marginal bands. The posterior median eyes are set far forward and are greatly enlarged, hence the common name.

Deinopis captures its prey by casting a rectangular, expandable web – made of cribellate silk – over it. The spider holds the four corners of the web with its front two pairs of legs while hanging head down a few centimetres above a horizontal surface. It is supported by a scaffolding of non-sticky silk. When the prey wanders beneath the waiting spider, the spider throws the web over it, much like the rete of a gladiator.

Deinopis makes its net after nightfall and awaits prey during the dark hours. During daytime, it may be found pressed flat against the bark of a branch or twig, with the long two pairs of front legs stretched forwards and the back four legs grasping the twig firmly.

Not a common spider, it has been collected from small bushes in KwaZulu-Natal and Mpumalanga and from fynbos in the Cape.

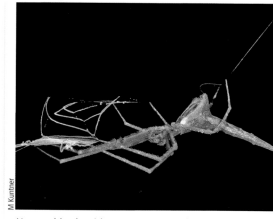

Humped-back spider, Menneus camelus, with the distinctive hump on its abdomen.

The distinctive eye pattern of Deinopis.

The eye pattern of Menneus camelus.

Humped-back spiders
GENUS: *Menneus*

HABITAT: In built-up areas; in trees; on bushes and plants and in low base vegetation; on or under grass; in forests
SIZE: Medium-large, 12 mm; female slightly larger than male
COLLECTING METHODS: Sweep-netting; beating; hand-to-jar; night collecting

The outstanding characteristic of *Menneus* is the presence of a large, single hump situated to one side of the female abdomen (in males, the abdomen is long and straight). The spider's colour, generally yellowish-brown, resembles the bark of the tree on which it rests during the daylight hours. It is covered in white hairs and mottled with brown markings. The eyes are in two rows, with the anterior row slightly procurved and the posterior row slightly recurved. Under magnification and seen from above, the front of the carapace looks not unlike the head of a barbel.

The prey capture method of *Menneus* is similar to that of *Deinopis*, except that *Menneus* is not reliant on prey walking beneath it. It tends to await its prey on grass stems and twigs near the ground. When prey comes within reach, the spider expands its net to five or six times its original size and hurls itself and the web upon it, from whatever angle.

A nocturnal hunter, *Menneus* begins spinning its catch web at twilight. It is found throughout southern Africa, but it is not common.

Camel-back spiders
GENUS: *Avellopsis*

> **HABITAT: On bushes and plants or in low base vegetation**
> **SIZE: Medium, 6–7 mm; female slightly larger than male**
> **COLLECTING METHODS: Sweep-netting; beating; hand-to-jar**

The only known species belonging to this genus, *Avellopsis capensis*, is found in the Western Cape. It is smaller than its cousins, but closely resembles *Menneus*: it has a similar colour and eye pattern, but a bulkier build. The carapace is distinctive in being wider over the thoracic area. The abdomen of both males and females presents with two humps.

A. *capensis* is found in scaffold webs low down among rocks and vegetation in coastal forests with winter rainfall.

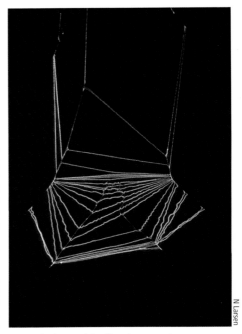

Expanded net of Avellopsis capensis.

Camel-back spider, Avellopsis capensis, *holding its net ready.*

Female Camel-back spider constructing her net.

Face of Avellopsis capensis.

Tube-web spider, Segestriidae ariadna.

Tube-web spiders

Tube-web spiders

FAMILY: Segestriidae

GENERA: *Ariadna*

> **LIFESTYLE: Sedentary, web-bound**
> **HABITAT: In built-up areas; on or under bark; in webbing, under stones; on rocks or in crevices of rocks; in and under leaf litter and rotting logs**
> **SIZE: Medium to medium-large, 6–15 mm**
> **ACTIVITY: Nocturnal**
> **DANGER: Harmless**
> **COLLECTING METHOD: Hand-to-jar**

Segestriid in its retreat with trip lines.

Segestriids have six eyes closely grouped in the centre front of the head. The cephalothorax is longer than it is wide and generally dark brown. Most species in southern Africa are rather drab and uniformly coloured in shades of brown. The long, oval abdomen is sometimes a greyish-brown. The abdomen is bulbous and tends to droop over to one side when the spider is removed from its retreat; this is because the pedicel is very thin and weak. Characteristic of this family is the third pair of legs, which is directed forwards instead of backwards. Segestriidae breathe through four tracheal spiracles and book lungs. They are haplogene spiders.

Nocturnal and sedentary, segestriids spend most of their lives in a tubular retreat of tough white silk under rocks, fallen logs, in crevices of rocks and often in the rolled-up dead leaves of succulent plants. In some species, single lines of silken thread radiate from the mouth of the tube, acting as trip lines to alert the spider of passing prey. The spider can be seen waiting within the tube with the first three pairs of legs projecting slightly.

Sheet- and Funnel-web spiders

Funnel-web spiders

FAMILY: Agelenidae

GENERA: *Olorunia* (Grass funnel-web spiders), *Benoitia, Mistaria, Tegenaria* (House funnel-web spiders)

> LIFESTYLE: **Sedentary, web-bound**
> HABITAT: **In built-up areas; on bushes and plants or in low base vegetation; on or under grass**
> SIZE: **Medium to medium-large, 8–12 mm**
> ACTIVITY: **Diurnal/Nocturnal**
> DANGER: **Harmless**
> COLLECTING METHOD: **Hand-to-jar**

The female Grass funnel-web spider, *Olorunia*, lives permanently on a large, sheet-like web with a funnel retreat made close to the substrate. In the field, it may be identified by its web and, once in the hand, by its resemblance to wolf spiders in size and colour

N Larsen

Male House funnel-web spider with moth.

(see p. 92). *Olorunia* is usually dark sooty-grey to mottled brown, and the abdomen is decorated with a reddish-brown folium and a series of yellow to white spots or bands. The legs are long, tapered and spiny. The carapace is long and narrowed in front. The eyes, which are nearly equal in size, are situated in two procurved rows. The abdomen is oval and tapers to the rear. Characteristic are the two elongated and slender posterior spinnerets, tapering at the ends and visible from above. The agelenids have three claws.

In *Tegenaria* the eyes are in two straight rows and the apical segment of the posterior pair of spinnerets is shorter.

M Filmer

Grass funnel-web spider, Olorunia punctata.

N Larsen

Female House funnel-web spider, Tegenaria domestica.

darker than the rest. The abdomen tends to be globose and is usually shiny black to brown, sometimes with white markings. In most of the species the legs are relatively long and thin. Linyphiids are often overlooked because of their small size and secluded, sedentary behaviour. Most of them build a distinctive web close to the ground – often a small sheet web – which may have strands of silken thread above it. Some species that live in low base vegetation build a superstructure above the sheet, with several central draw lines pulling the centre of the sheet web up slightly. This has given rise to the common name Hammock spider. The webs are best seen when covered with early-morning dew.

The spider lives and runs on the underside of the web, which is used as a food trap. When prey falls on the sheet, the spider grabs it, pulls it through the web and devours it on the substrate.

DWARF OR MONEY SPIDERS

SUBFAMILY: Erigoninae

GENERA: 12 including *Erigone, Erigonops, Ostearius*

> **LIFESTYLE: Sedentary, web-bound; free-running, ground-living**
> **HABITAT: On bushes and plants or in low base vegetation; in and under leaf litter and rotting logs; on the seashore**
> **SIZE: Tiny to small, <3.5 mm**
> **ACTIVITY: Diurnal/Nocturnal**

Most Dwarf spiders are less than 2 mm long. They can be distinguished from the Linyphiinae in having shorter, more robust legs and being very dark brown to black and shiny. In the males of some species, the front part of the carapace is grossly (and extravagantly) deformed.

Dwarf spiders make tiny, flat sheet webs close to the soil, often in depressions made by animal hooves, for example. Some live under debris and leaf litter. A species of *Erigonops* is found in unoccupied worm tubes between the tidal marks on the shores of the Cape Peninsula.

Ostearius melanopygius is a cosmopolitan species commonly found in southern Africa.

Long-legged cave spiders

FAMILY: Telemidae

GENUS: *Cangoderces*

> **LIFESTYLE: Sedentary, web-bound**
> **HABITAT: In caves**
> **SIZE: Tiny to very small, <2 mm**
> **ACTIVITY: Nocturnal**
> **DANGER: Harmless**
> **COLLECTING METHODS: Hand-to-jar; pooter**

The telemids are tiny, six-eyed spiders, always found in dark places. Some species have lost most of their coloration and present a pale yellow, almost translucent colour. *Cangoderces* is pale, with only the articulations of the leg segments, the sternum

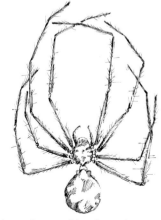

Long-legged cave spider, Cangoderces.

and the chelicerae a light reddish-brown. The carapace and abdomen are chitinous.

The cephalothorax and abdomen of telemids appear round from above, the abdomen itself being quite globose. The legs are long, slender and well covered with setae, and point outwards and forwards. The eyes are minute and are difficult to see without magnification, as they lack pigmentation. They are set on slightly raised tubercles in three widely separated groups of two, forming a recurved line.

Virtually nothing is known about the behaviour of these small spiders. Specimens collected in the Cango Caves were found in small webs spun in crevices in the rock wall, always about 45 cm above the ground.

Cob-web spiders

Cave cob-web spiders

FAMILY: Nesticidae

GENUS: *Nesticella*

> **LIFESTYLE: Sedentary, web-bound**
> **HABITAT: In webbing under stones; in and under leaf litter and rotting logs; in forests; in caves**
> **SIZE: Small, 3–5 mm**
> **ACTIVITY: Diurnal/Nocturnal**
> **DANGER: Harmless**
> **COLLECTING METHOD: Hand-to-jar**

Nesticidae are small spiders resembling Theridiidae (see p. 68), but they have more robust legs. The first pair of legs is significantly longer than the other three pairs. The diameter of the legs is uniform throughout their length. The embolus of the male pedipalp is loosely arranged with processes on the cymbium, unlike the compact embolus of male theridiids.

Nesticella often constructs its web in caves.

Living in dark, dank places and under damp stones, some species have lost their pigmentation. This is first seen in the often rudimentary eyes. The abdomen is greyish and pale or yellowish-white; in some species it is covered with short, fluffy brown hairs.

Little is known about the behaviour of these small spiders. They make a fine web under damp stones or in dark, dank places, and are well adapted to life in caves. The web is similar to those made by *Steatoda* (see p. 68), hence the family's common name.

The female carries the egg sac, which is attached to the spinnerets (similar to Wolf spiders – see p. 92). The egg sac is pale brown.

Daddy longlegs spiders

FAMILY: Pholcidae

GENERA: *Artema, Pholcus, Smeringopus, Spermophora, Ninetis, Quamtana*

> **LIFESTYLE: Sedentary, web-bound**
> **HABITAT: In built-up areas; on rocks or in crevices of rocks; in and under leaf litter and rotting logs; in disused holes; in caves**
> **SIZE: Very small to medium-large, 2–10 mm (leg span up to 30 mm)**
> **ACTIVITY: Nocturnal**
> **DANGER: Harmless**
> **COLLECTING METHOD: Hand-to-jar**

Daddy longlegs spider in its web.

Pholcidae are delicate spiders with very thin, long legs – as much as four times longer than the body – that lack setae. *Pholcus* and *Smeringopus* usually have a cylindrical abdomen with chevron markings, while *Spermophora* usually has a more globose abdomen. The eye patterns of *Pholcus* and *Smeringopus* are similar: there are two sets of three contiguous eyes on either side of the carapace, which are raised on slight tubercles, with two smaller anterior median eyes in the centre front of the carapace. In *Spermophora* the anterior median eyes are absent.

These long-legged, often-seen spiders spin a simple web of long threads that crisscross in an irregular fashion. They are mostly seen in dark corners of garages, disused habitations, damp places and the disused holes of mammals. The webs are frequently covered with dust and debris.

The spider hangs upside-down towards the centre of the web. Sometimes, however, the web appears to be more concentrated away from the centre, and this is where the spider will be found. The apparent size of the web can sometimes be misleading, as offspring setting up home nearby create a continuation of the main web.

Pholcids, unlike Violin spiders (see p. 101), remain on their webs unless torn away from them when supporting structures such as garage rubble or building material are moved. When detached from the web, they appear to bounce along the floor as they search for a hiding place. If the web is touched or blown upon, the spider will shake itself and the web violently, or swing itself around rapidly. The vibration that these movements cause makes the spider difficult to see among the irregular strands of its web.

The female pholcid carries the eggs – loosely joined together with sticky silk – in her chelicerae.

Preying on ants and other household pests, these spiders are to be treasured in the home, certainly never killed.

Female Smeringopus pallidus *carrying an egg sac.*

Comb-footed spiders

FAMILY: Theridiidae

GENERA: 15 including *Argyrodes,*
Latrodectus, Steatoda, Theridion

> LIFESTYLE: Sedentary, web-bound
> HABITAT: In built-up areas; in trees;
> in webbing under stones; on rocks
> or in crevices of rocks; on bushes and
> plants or in low base vegetation;
> on or under grass; in and under leaf
> litter and rotting logs; in forests; in
> other spiders' webs; in disused holes
> SIZE: Very small to large, 2–16 mm
> ACTIVITY: Diurnal/Nocturnal
> DANGER: Venomous
> COLLECTING METHOD: Hand-to-jar

Theridiids are very small to large spiders. They
have a globose abdomen and long legs, of
which the third pair is the shortest. They are
sedentary and when at rest, hang upside-
down in their webs. They have comb-like
setae on the tarsi of the fourth pair of legs,
which consist of a row of six to 10 modified
hairs. These setae are used to fling out the
silk over the prey at capture.

The most infamous member of this vast
family is the Black button spider. *Latrodectus
indistinctus, L. cinctus, L. karooensis* and
L. renivulvatus fall into this species complex.
Black button spiders are some of the most
dangerous spiders in southern Africa. These
spiders have a neurotoxic venom, which
affects both the heart and respiratory
system. The bite is painful and produces
symptoms within half an hour, which
include anxiety, severe chest and abdominal
pains, headache, rapid changes in body
temperature and coldness of the skin. At
the site of the bite a red, inflamed swelling
forms, and often a rash appears. Although
these symptoms are alarming, no deaths
have been recorded in southern Africa in
the last six decades. Antivenom is available
from the South African Institute for Medical
Research in Johannesburg.

As their common name suggests, Black
button spiders are black. They are medium is
size. Most species have some form of orange-
red marking (or markings) on the dorsal side
of the abdomen, although this is absent
in some adult females. Only juvenile Black
button spiders have red markings on the

Black button spider with egg sac.

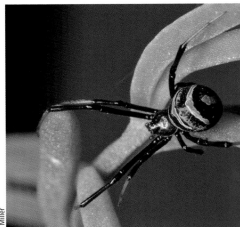

Juvenile Latrodectus renivulvatus.

Pale-coloured Latrodectus geometricus.

ventral side of the abdomen. (The American *L. mactans* has a bright red hourglass marking ventrally.) They are sedentary and usually found in the field; they are not common in populated areas.

L. geometricus (Geometric button spider) and *L. rhodesiensis* (Rhodesian button spider) are commonly known as Brown button spiders. They show the characteristic hourglass pattern on the ventral side of the abdomen. Geometric button spiders may vary in colour from cream, a dirty green and brown to pitch black with geometric patterns on the dorsal side of the abdomen. The Geometric button spider is found in abundance in and around human habitation, especially outbuildings, garages, verandas and under window ledges. The Rhodesian button spider is found in grasslands and bush country (also around houses), but it is not common in South Africa.

Latrodectus species may be difficult to tell apart. However, their egg sacs are a strong diagnostic feature. The Black button spider makes a smooth, round, whitish-yellow egg sac about 10 mm in diameter, and the web normally contains more than one. The web of *L. geometricus* also commonly houses

more than one egg sac, but these are slightly smaller and always spiky and irregular in shape. *L. rhodesiensis* makes an impressive cluster of four or five large, fluffy balls of soft outer silk. When held up to the light, the smaller, more dense ball containing the eggs can be seen within each fluffy outer covering.

Steatoda (False button spider) is often mistaken for a Black or Brown button spider. However, on close examination the spider can be seen to be brown or black with no markings ventrally, and with a cream-white marking on the anterior dorsal aspect of the abdomen. Males may be confused with

Geometric button spider, Latrodectus geometricus, *in its web.*

False button spider, Steatoda capensis.

False house button spider, Theridion delicatum.

Detail of comb on fourth tarsus of all Theridiids.

Egg sacs of Latrodectus geometricus, L. indistinctus *and* L. rhodesiensis.

Male Dew-drop spider, Argyrodes.

those of *Latrodectus* but have a distinctive scute, or shield, behind the pedicel on the front of the abdomen.

Theridion (False house button spider) is smaller than the true button spiders (never more than 5–6 mm) and generally has a creamy brown to dark brown abdomen with irregular markings. Its legs appear to be striped. This small spider is commonly found in houses and forests.

Argyrodes (Dew-drop spider) is a small, often silver-coloured spider. It is kleptoparasitic, as it lives in the webs of other spiders, especially those of *Argiope*, *Cyrtophora* (see pp. 33 and 39) and *Nephila* (see p. 42), where it eats discarded prey remains. The males of some *Argyrodes* have enlarged, deformed protuberances at the front of the carapace, similar to some male

linyphiids (see p. 64). In some species the abdomen is long and tail-like in appearance.

Theridiids make many different kinds of web. Some build a web with an irregular network of strong threads without any apparent design (commonly called cob webs). Others build scaffold webs, which form a three-dimensional trellis of silken threads. Drop lines run from the lower mantle of the web to the ground or substrate; often, knockdown lines of strong silk attach the upper part of the mantle to leaves, branches or other overhead attachment points. The design of the drop lines depends on whether the spider wants to capture flying or crawling prey. If the former, then droplets of sticky silk are deposited about halfway up the lines; if the latter, the sticky droplets are placed on the lines near to the ground. The upper knockdown lines knock flying insects onto the mantle, where capture is made.

Some of the species make a retreat with a ventral opening centred in the web, while others, such as *Latrodectus*, have retreats to the side of the web. Some of the smaller species do not make webs of their own but live in and around the webs of other spiders.

Many of the theridiid species tend to be sedentary and do not leave their intricate webs once they have been built.

N Larsen

Drymusa capensis *with captured* Theridion delicatum.

False violin spiders

FAMILY: Drymusidae

GENUS: *Drymusa*

> **LIFESTYLE: Sedentary, web-bound**
> **HABITAT: In caves; under logs; among**
> **rocks and leaf litter in forests**
> **SIZE: Small to medium-large, 4.5–15 mm**
> **ACTIVITY: Nocturnal**
> **DANGER: Harmless**
> **COLLECTING METHODS: Hand-to-jar;**
> **sifting; pooter**

Previously placed under the family Scytodidae, these small to medium-large brown spiders have long, slender legs like *Scytodes* (see p. 100). However, *Drymusa* is different in having a depressed carapace with a dark V-shaped pattern and a much wider clypeus.

The six eyes are arranged in three diads and the chelicerae are fused at the base. Simple genitalia are evident and a colulus is easily seen, especially in the females.

Two features that distinguish *Drymusa* from another previous Scytodid, *Loxosceles* (now incorporated in the family Sicariidae; see p. 100) is that it has three claws and it lives in cob webs, as opposed to two claws in the cursorial *Loxosceles*.

Little is known about the behaviour of *Drymusa*. From observations it is clear that it actively catches prey in its web; prey is not caught using the web itself. If the prey is small, it is caught with the chelicerae. Larger prey is first wrapped in silk and then bitten.

Drymusa has been collected in coastal forests, often in leaf litter or in pholcid-like cob webs under logs, among rocks and in caves.

Free-living web invaders

Pirate spiders

FAMILY: Mimetidae

GENERA: *Ero, Mimetus*

> LIFESTYLE: Free-running, plant-living
> HABITAT: In other spiders' webs
> SIZE: Small to medium, 3–7 mm
> ACTIVITY: Nocturnal
> DANGER: Harmless
> COLLECTING METHODS: Sweep-netting; beating; hand-to-jar; night collecting

Pirate spider, Mimetus sp.

Ero *with captured spider.*

Spines on the tarsus of Mimetidae spiders.

Spiders from the Mimetidae family are easily identified by the characteristic spines on the long first two pairs of legs, and the distinctively marked triangular to globose abdomen. They are araneophagus and hunt in the webs of other spiders, and are unique in that they prey exclusively on other web-living spiders.

Some authors place Mimetidae with the hunters; however, they are sluggish when compared to the free-runners. The mimetid climbs surreptitiously onto the webs of other spiders, mainly theridiids (see p. 68), agenelids and orb weavers such as *Araneus* (see p. 35). It usually rests during the day, and becomes active at dusk and dawn – as Lawrence (1981) puts it, 'the most fitting hours for the assassin and terrorist'. As night falls, it begins to pluck at and vibrate its victim's web and, when the inhabitant comes to investigate, the mimetid stretches its armed forelegs up, forwards and over the host, pulling it down. It quickly bites into the femur of the first leg of its prey and, according to Lawrence, 'death is almost instantaneous'. The empty shell of the dead spider is left hanging in its own snare.

Spurred orb-weavers

FAMILY: Mysmenidae

GENUS: *Isela*

> LIFESTYLE: Free-running, plant-living
> HABITAT: In other spiders' webs
> SIZE: Tiny to very small, 0.5–2 mm
> ACTIVITY: Diurnal/Nocturnal
> DANGER: Harmless
> COLLECTING METHODS: Hand-to-jar; pooter

The spiders in this family were recently removed from the family Symphytognathidae (see p. 47). They are tiny, unsclerotized spiders with a spherical abdomen, eight eyes and three tarsal claws. Kleptoparasites, they have been found living on the sheet webs of the diplurid spider *Allothele* (see p. 115), where they feed on abandoned prey.

Free-living ground spiders

Seashore spiders

FAMILY: Anyphaenidae

GENUS: *Amaurobioides* (African seashore spiders)

LIFESTYLE: **Free-running, ground-living**
HABITAT: **On the seashore**
SIZE: **Medium-large to large, 13–17 mm; female larger than male**
ACTIVITY: **Diurnal/Nocturnal**
DANGER: **Harmless**
COLLECTING METHOD: **Hand-to-jar**

Dark reddish-brown, *Amaurobioides* has robust legs. The body is covered with fine hairs known as hydrofuge setae. The legs are not armed with spines and have two claws. The eyes are situated on a low protuberance in a group spread across half the carapace width. The chelicerae are stout, almost bulbous, and the fangs are strong. The abdomen has a distinctive black-brown chevron pattern on the dorsal aspect.

The anyphaenids live along the coast of the Eastern and Western Cape, restricted to beaches where rocky faces are present. They live within the coastline's splash zone, between the high-water neap and high-water spring tide delimitations. Unlike Long-jawed intertidal spiders (see p. 82), they become submerged only during spring tides.

In areas with strong wave action, they make a web-lined nest under a limpet shell or in an empty barnacle, closing it completely during the spring tide. The lining is made of strong silk and is watertight; enough oxygen is sealed in for prolonged immersion. In areas with weak wave action, the spiders do

N Larsen

African seashore spider, Amaurobioides africana.

not build nests, but with the help of their hydrofuge setae trap enough air around their bodies to supply them with oxygen during their period of submersion.

When not submerged, *Amaurobioides* roams around the rocks in search of prey, which consists mainly of various intertidal arthropods.

These spiders are found only in the southern hemisphere, and only one species, *A. africana*, has been recorded in the region.

Sand divers and Termite hunters

FAMILY: Ammoxenidae

GENERA: *Ammoxenus* (Sand divers), *Rastellus* (Termite hunters)

> LIFESTYLE: Free-running, ground-living
> HABITAT: On or under sand; on open ground; in semi-arid desert; in association with termites
> SIZE: Small to medium, 1.3–10 mm
> ACTIVITY: Diurnal
> DANGER: Harmless
> COLLECTING METHODS: Hand-to-jar; pitfall trap

Extremely fast and agile, ammoxenids are not often seen. They are adapted to life in sandy soils, especially the mounds of fine, sandy grains made by termites. *Ammoxenus* is covered with dense, recumbent, plumose hairs, giving them a greasy appearance. The abdomen is oval in shape; in most species, cream-coloured markings run down the sides and middle of the dorsal aspect. The legs are long and covered with hairs. The tarsi are very long and flexible. The tarsi of *Rastellus* is not flexible. The eyes are arranged in a compact group on a small protuberance on the front of the carapace. The chelicerae are modified for burrowing.

Sand-diving spider, Ammoxenus amphalodes.

Sand-diving spider, Ammoxenus *sp.*

Ammoxenidae are usually found around the nests of termites, their favourite prey. When foraging, *Ammoxenus* travels rapidly over the ground. It even more rapidly dives into the sand head first if disturbed or threatened. During non-active periods, you may find it concealed in the soil mounds of termites, where it covers itself with a thin layer of slightly sticky silk. *Rastellus* constructs silk-lined burrows close to termite nests.

Female spiders conceal their egg sacs, which resemble cups, in the soil mound.

Ammoxenidae are found throughout southern Africa but their association with termites affects their distribution from region to region.

Long-neck spiders

FAMILY: Archaeidae

GENERA: *Eriauchenius, Afrarchaea*
(African long-necked spiders)

> LIFESTYLE: Free-running, ground-living
> HABITAT: In scrapes or free-running,
> under stones; on open ground; in
> and under leaf litter and rotting logs;
> in forests
> SIZE: Small to medium, 3–7 mm
> ACTIVITY: Diurnal/Nocturnal
> DANGER: Harmless
> COLLECTING METHODS: Hand-to-jar;
> pitfall trap; tullgren funnel; sifting;
> rock turning

The archaeids are rare, small and strange-
looking araneophagus spiders, easily recognized
under magnification by the cephalic region of
the carapace, which is raised high above the
thoracic region; hence the common name.

The surface of the reddish-brown carapace
is covered with small, flattened protuberances,
each with a short, thick, white seta. The anterior
median eyes are large and dark; the other eyes
are smaller and paler in colour. The chelicerae
are much enlarged, long and slender, with
the fangs short and curved. The legs are also
reddish-brown and are long and slender, with
the first pair the longest and the third pair the
shortest. The abdomen is globular, with patches

Male Woods' long-neck spider,
Afrarchaea woodae.

Eriauchenius gracilicollus *from Madagascar,
showing its long neck.*

of chitinous tissue covered overall with setae.
The male has a scute on the anterior dorsal part
of the abdomen.

Slow-moving hunters, Long-neck spiders
do not construct a snare or retreat. They are
cryptozoic and live in damp places such as in
leaf litter and under stones, and have been
observed feeding on other spiders. Although
they have a reasonably wide distribution in
forests in the eastern parts of southern Africa,
they are seldom found, even when collectors
specifically search for them.

Orange lungless spiders

FAMILY: Caponiidae

GENERA: *Caponia* (Eight-eyed orange
lungless spiders), *Diploglena* (Two-
eyed orange lungless spiders)

> LIFESTYLE: Free-running, ground-
> living
> HABITAT: In webbing, scrapes
> or free-running, under stones; on
> open ground; in semi-arid desert
> SIZE: Medium to medium-large,
> 6–13 mm; female slightly larger
> than male
> ACTIVITY: Diurnal/Nocturnal
> DANGER: Harmless
> COLLECTING METHODS: Hand-to-jar;
> pitfall trap; rock turning

The caponiids are easily recognized by the deep yellow to orange colour of the legs and carapace. They have no book lungs and breathe through two pairs of tracheae situated on the anterior of the abdomen. *Diploglena* has two eyes, while *Caponia* has eight. The carapace is shield-like, like that of the palpimanids (see p. 95), but the first pair of legs is not thick and robust. The abdomen, oval in shape, is pale yellow to grey, and clothed in fine black hairs. The legs have no true spines. The tarsi have three claws.

Lungless spiders do not build webs. They are swift runners and pursue their prey over the ground. The spiders catch and overpower prey with their strong chelicerae and robust legs. They hide under stones, where they make a small, oval retreat of transparent silk. *Diploglena* is rare; only one species, *D. capensis*, is found in the drier parts of the Western Cape and Namibia. Various species of *Caponia* are found in most parts of southern Africa.

Sac spiders

FAMILY: Clubionidae

GENERA: *Clubiona* (Leaf-curling sac spiders), *Carteroniella* (Ant mimic spiders)

> **LIFESTYLE: Free-running, ground-living; free-running, plant-living**
> **HABITAT: On or under bark; in webbing, scrapes or free-running, under stones; on bushes and plants or in low base vegetation; on flowers or leaves; in and under leaf litter and rotting logs; in forests**
> **SIZE: Small to medium-large, 5–12 mm**
> **ACTIVITY: Diurnal/Nocturnal**
> **DANGER: Harmless**
> **COLLECTING METHODS: Sweep-netting; beating; hand-to-jar; pitfall trap**

Clubionidae are two-clawed spiders that resemble the miturgids (see p. 79) and gnaphosids (see p. 84) in general appearance, but lack the gnaphosids' characteristic spinnerets. They have a characteristic compact body coloured in various shades of cream, light brown and yellow.

Clubionids have long legs, with the scopulae on the tarsi dark brown or black. The chelicerae are long, rather stout and light brown. Some species have chevron markings on the abdomen. The eyes are small, almost

N Larsen

Eight-eyed orange lungless spider, Caponia capensis.

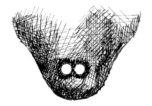

Eye pattern of Diploglena.

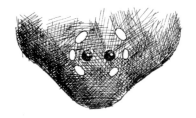

Eye pattern of Caponia.

N Larsen

Leaf-curling sac spider, Clubiona caplandensis.

the same size, and situated in two rows. Unlike the miturgid *Cheiracanthium*, *Clubiona* lacks a black face, and the first and fourth pairs of legs are equal in size.

Ground-living sac spiders include a group of medium-sized, dark-coloured spiders with slender legs and hard, often granular, integument. Arboreal clubionids live mostly on herbaceous plants, where they feed on pests.

Sac spiders are free-roaming, aggressive hunters. They catch their prey with great speed and agility, leaping on it and grabbing it with outstretched front legs.

Most members of this family construct tubular or flat sacs of dense white silk – either open at the ends or closed – to use as retreats. *Clubiona* makes a sac in rolled-up leaves, in folded blades of grass or under loose bark.

Carteroniella is an ant mimic; otherwise, little is known about this South African genus.

Dark sac spiders and Ant mimic sac spiders

FAMILY: Corinnidae

GENERA: 20 including *Apochinomma, Castianeira, Corinnomma, Graptartia, Cetonana, Spinotrachelas, Thysanana, Trachelas* (Ant mimic sac spiders), *Austrophaea, Copa, Corinna, Hortipes, Medmassa, Merenius* (Dark sac spiders)

LIFESTYLE: Free-running, ground-living
HABITAT: On the ground; under stones; in and under leaf litter and logs; in low base vegetation (grass and shrubs); in forests; in deserts
SIZE: Small to medium-large, 3–11 mm
ACTIVITY: Nocturnal
DANGER: Harmless
COLLECTING METHODS: Hand-to-jar; pitfall trap

Dark sac spider, Merenius alberti.

Ant mimic sac spider, Apochinomma *sp.*

The Corinnidae, formerly a subfamily of the Clubionidae, is a family of two-clawed, eight-eyed spiders with prominent claw tufts. Corinnids are dark in colour and usually have a sclerotized, granular integument with slender to sturdy legs. The males usually have an abdominal scute and are often more robustly built than the females. The first pair of legs usually have ventral cusps, setae or spines.

The family is divided into three subfamilies: Castianeirinae and Trachelinae (Ant mimic sac spiders); and Corinninae (Dark sac spiders). Certain genera are incorrectly placed in this family; a revision is underway.

Ant mimic sac spiders range in colour from yellow-brown, bright orange and dark-brown to metallic, with cream to black abdomens. They run with the front legs held aloft like antennae, and with the abdomen bobbing up and down. Like ants, they run with rapid, jerky movements and stop frequently. Prey is run down and captured with the anterior legs. *Graptartia* is different from its ant mimic family: it is yellow-brown to red-brown, and has a black abdomen with cream spots and triangular markings. It more resembles mutillid wasps in appearance and behaviour. *Trachelas* is similar in appearance and movement to the slow-moving Palpimanidae (see p. 95).

Copa and other Dark sac spiders are similar in appearance and behaviour to the Lycosidae and Miturgidae.

Corinnids can be collected from silk retreats in curled leaves, from under bark or in leaf litter. Round to oval egg sacs are constructed from white silk and attached to the substrate.

Spiny-legged sac spiders

FAMILY: Liocranidae

GENERA: *Andromma, Argistes, Coryssiphus, Rhaeboctesis*

> LIFESTYLE: Free-running, ground-living
> HABITAT: On the ground; under stones; in ground litter; in forests
> SIZE: Small to medium-large, 3–15 mm
> ACTIVITY: Nocturnal
> DANGER: Harmless
> COLLECTING METHODS: Hand-to-jar; pitfall trap

Liocranidae is a family of two-clawed, eight-eyed spiders without claw tufts. The first two pairs of legs have numerous pairs of ventral spines on the tibiae and metatarsi.

C Haddad

Spiny-legged sac spider, Rhaeboctesis *sp.*

Liocranids were formerly a subfamily of Clubionidae, but unlike Clubionidae, they lack claw tufts. They vary in colour from brown, shades of yellow or red to brown and black, with or without low contrast abdominal patterns. Liocranids resemble lycosids and corinnids, while *Andromma* mimics ants or termites. Not much is known about liocranid biology. They are a diverse family occurring from forest to desert habitats.

The three subfamilies – Cybaeodinae, Liocraninae and Phurolithinae – are in need of revision.

Prowling sac spiders

FAMILY: Miturgidae

GENERA: *Cheiracanthium* (Long-legged sac spiders), *Cheiramiona* (Long-legged sac spiders), *Parapostenus* (Long legged sac spiders)

**LIFESTYLE: Free-running, ground-living; free-running, plant-living
HABITAT: On or under bark; in webbing, scrapes or free-running, under stones; on bushes and plants or in low base vegetation; on flowers** or leaves; in and under leaf litter and rotting logs; in forests
**SIZE: Small to medium-large, 3–12.5 mm
ACTIVITY: Nocturnal
DANGER: Venomous
COLLECTING METHODS: Sweep-netting; beating; hand-to-jar; pitfall trap**

Miturgidae are two-clawed spiders that resemble the clubionids (see p. 76) in general appearance. They have long legs, and the scopulae on the tarsi are dark brown or black. The chelicerae are long, rather stout and black. Some species have chevron markings on the abdomen. The eyes are small, almost the same size, and situated in two rows.

In *Cheiracanthium* and *Cheiramiona*, the first pair of legs are the longest, while in clubionids, the first and fourth pairs of legs are equal in size. The defining characteristic of *Cheiracanthium furculatum* is its black face. *Cheiramiona* has a sepia chevron pattern on the abdomen's dorsal aspect and a dark ventral mark. In *Cheiracanthium*, the chevron is absent or indistinct and the ventral mark is always absent.

N Larsen

Long-legged sac spider,
Cheiracanthium furculatum.

Diagnostic black face of Cheiracanthium furculatum.

Sac spiders are free-roaming, aggressive hunters. They catch prey with great speed and agility, leaping on it and grabbing it with outstretched front legs.

Cheiracanthium furculatum, which is often found inside houses, makes a flattened, disc-shaped sac in the folds of curtains, behind and under objects and in cupboards. The sacs are very tough and papery and shiny in appearance. The egg sac is similar but smaller.

Being wanderers at night, these spiders often move over sleeping humans and, being aggressive, will bite at the slightest provocation. The bites are painless, and occur most often on the face and neck or hands. The bites are characterized by two bite marks approximately 6 mm apart. The venom is cytotoxic. Within 24 hours, the site becomes inflamed and swollen, and it ulcerates after a few days. The ulcerative wound is very slow to heal and poses a risk of secondary infection. Accompanying fever and malaise may be present, often with severe headache. *C. furculatum* is the species known to inflict bites with significant consequences.

Forest floor and Ground spiders

FAMILY: Zoropsidae

GENERA: *Griswoldia, Phanotea*

> **LIFESTYLE: Free-running, ground-living**
> **HABITAT: In and under leaf litter and rotting logs; in forests; in caves**
> **SIZE: Medium to medium-large, 6–15 mm**
> **ACTIVITY: Nocturnal**
> **DANGER: Harmless**
> **COLLECTING METHODS: Hand-to-jar; pitfall trap; tullgren funnel; sifting**

Griswoldia and *Phanotea* were recently removed from the Miturgidae family and placed in the Zoropsidae family.

This family includes spiders with two or three tarsal claws, with or without a cribellum. In our region only one subfamily, Griswoldiinae, has been recorded. The spiders in this subfamily have only two claws and lack a cribellum.

Forest floor spider, Phanotea ceratogyna.

Meikle's forest floor spider,
Griswoldia meikleae.

Griswoldia (formerly known as *Machadonia*) and *Phanotea* are cryptozoic spiders that live in the damp humus of forests. They are short-legged, robust spiders, superficially resembling *Lycosa* (see p. 92) and *Ctenus* (see p. 81). Their colour varies from reddish-brown to dark brown, with the carapace of *Griswoldia* showing dark lateral bands. *Phanotea* has a dark carapace, and the abdomen shows faint markings ranging from spots to chevrons. Twenty-five species are known from the Western Cape, Eastern Cape, KwaZulu-Natal and Limpopo.

The eyes of *Phanotea* are small in comparison with the large carapace. The anterior row is slightly recurved; the posterior row is straight or recurved. The maxillae are large and robust. The legs have numerous long and strong spines and, compared to those of other cave dwellers, are large.

Three species of *Phanotea* have adapted to cave life. Very little is known about this species. All of the other 24 species are cursorial and live in forest humus and leaf litter. Like other hunters, *Phanotea* runs down and overpowers prey with speed and agility.

Griswoldia and *Phanotea* are endemic to southern Africa.

Tropical wolf spiders

FAMILY: Ctenidae

GENERA: *Africactenus, Anahita, Ctenus*

LIFESTYLE: Free-running, ground-living
HABITAT: Free-running, under stones; on rocks or in crevices of rocks; in and under leaf litter and rotting logs; in forests
SIZE: Medium to very large, 5–40 mm
ACTIVITY: Nocturnal
DANGER: Harmless. It has been found that the bite of some South American species has a neurotoxic effect on man. Ctenids should therefore be handled with care.
COLLECTING METHODS: Hand-to-jar; night collecting; pitfall trap; rock turning

In general, the smaller ctenids resemble Wolf spiders (see p. 92), and the larger ctenids resemble Huntsman spiders (see p. 88). The coloration of Ctenidae camouflages these spiders in their natural habitat. Their long legs are similar to those of the sparassids, but they do not pull them back when at rest, as

Tropical wolf spider, Anahita.

Eye pattern of Ctenidae.

Ctenidae in a threatening pose.

the sparassids do. The legs are strong with stout spines, and the tarsi have two claws and scopulae. The eyes are similar to the lycosids, but the anterior eye row is strongly recurved.

Ctenidae are wandering hunters and do not make webs. They often hold the front pair of legs high off the ground as they move rapidly over the undergrowth in search of prey. They are aggressive and will attack at the slightest provocation. When threatened, the spider sits back, raises the first two pairs of legs high above the head, and pushes the chelicerae forward.

They are found in the leaves of forest humus and in the cracks of rock formations. The smaller species are common in and about the humus of compost heaps in gardens. Here, a ctenid may be passed off as 'just another Wolf spider'!

Long-jawed intertidal spiders

FAMILY: Desidae

GENUS: *Desis*

LIFESTYLE: Free-running, ground-living
HABITAT: On the seashore
SIZE: Large, 18–20 mm (chelicerae included)
ACTIVITY: Diurnal/Nocturnal
DANGER: Harmless
COLLECTING METHOD: Hand-to-jar

Desidae are formidable-looking spiders with a uniform greyish-brown body and brown cephalothorax. Growing up to 20 mm in length, they have greatly enlarged chelicerae and fangs that project forwards; these alone make up about one third of the spider's total length. The legs are well developed and stubby, designed for gripping firmly onto rocks. These spiders live at the lower levels of the flooding area and are therefore subjected to rigorous wave action. *Desis formidabilis*, the only known southern African species, is slightly larger than the other intertidal spider in the region, *Amaurobioides africana* (see p. 73). It has special aquatic adaptations to survive in its chosen habitat.

N Larsen

Long-jawed intertidal spider, Desis formidabilis.

Long-fanged six-eyed intertidal spider, Dysdera crocata.

Desis lives along rocky shores, favouring the area between the normal low and high tide marks. It is subjected to frequent periods of flooding (it is submerged every day) and more rigorous wave action. It builds its retreat in a place that offers good protection, such as a deserted limpet shell or a crack in a rock. As such sites are often in short supply, the spiders vie with one another for the use of them, smaller spiders often being evicted by larger ones. The retreat is lined with waterproof webbing, but if the retreat does become flooded, the air adhering to the spider's waxy hairs will supply it with oxygen until the next low tide.

When its habitat is not flooded, *Desis* emerges to forage. It roams in search of its intertidal arthropod prey which, because of the niche occupied by *Desis*, differs from that of *Amaurobioides*. There is some competition, however, and if the spiders meet and confront each other, *Desis* is usually the victor.

Long-fanged six-eyed spiders

FAMILY: Dysderidae

GENUS: *Dysdera*

LIFESTYLE: Free-running, ground-living
HABITAT: In webbing, scrapes or free-running, under stones; on open ground
SIZE: Medium-large, 10–12 mm; female slightly larger than male
ACTIVITY: Nocturnal
DANGER: Harmless
COLLECTING METHODS: Hand-to-jar; night collecting; pitfall trap; rock turning

Dysdera has a bright reddish-brown, ovoid, smooth carapace and a pale cream abdomen. The robust legs, which bear spines, are reddish-brown, and there are two tarsal claws with dense claw tufts. The chelicerae are large and

Flat-bellied ground spider, Camillina *sp.*

porrect and armed with long fangs. The six light-coloured eyes are arranged in a compact group close to the front of the carapace.

Dysderids do not build snares. They are free-running, solitary spiders. They live under stones and other rubble, where they make a flattened oval retreat of tough silk. In the heat of day they remain hidden, emerging at night to hunt. The exceptionally large chelicerae and fangs allow the spider to catch and eat woodlice, a prey not easily taken by most other spiders.

Only the cosmopolitan *Dysdera crocata* occurs in South Africa.

Flat-bellied ground spiders

FAMILY: Gnaphosidae

GENERA: 31 including *Drassodes, Asemesthes, Callilepis, Setaphis, Zelotes, Micaria*

> **LIFESTYLE: Free-running, ground-living**
> **HABITAT: In built-up areas; on or under bark; in webbing, scrapes or free-running, under stones; in and under leaf litter and rotting logs**
> **SIZE: Small to large, 3–17 mm**

> **ACTIVITY: Diurnal/Nocturnal**
> **DANGER: Harmless**
> **COLLECTING METHODS: Hand-to-jar; night collecting; pitfall trap; rock turning**

Gnaphosidae are dull-coloured spiders, ranging from grey to dark brown or black. Some genera have markings on the abdomen, which is clothed with fine hairs; hence the alternate common name – Mouse spiders. Sometimes the hairs may have a metallic sheen.

Gnaphosidae is a large family of more than 200 species. Some have an ovoid carapace while others have a narrow and oblong carapace. The eyes are in two rows – commonly both procurved – with the posterior median eyes in some species oval and set at an angle. The chelicerae are robust, but more slender than those of the Clubionidae (see p. 76). Gnaphosids tend to have a long, slightly flattened abdomen and characteristic cylindrical spinnerets. The spinnerets are markedly parallel to and separate from each other.

Flat-bellied ground spiders build small, irregular nests with their strong, sheet-like

Common rain spider, Palystes superciliosus.

Rock huntsman spider, Eusparassus *species.*

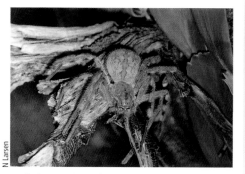

Cederberg rain spider, Palystes martinfilmeri.

Karoo rain spider, Parapalystes *species.*

pairs of legs are raised high above the head.

Palystes, the most commonly seen genus, tends to be a light to medium brown spider and has often been mistaken for one of the Baboon spiders (see p. 119). The clypeus of *Palystes* shows a white band, rather like a white moustache. Its abdomen may be unmarked or, as in the similar *Parapalystes,* it may have a indistinct brown, shield-shaped chevron pattern distinct in *Parapalystes.* The undersides of the legs show bands of yellow to darkish orange at the leg joints. A brush of red scopulae on the chelicerae is displayed to deter aggressors: when the spider raises its legs, it pushes the chelicerae forwards.

Olios is a smaller green spider with white to cream decorations on the abdomen to match its plant-living lifestle. *Eusparassus* is similar to *Olios* and is usually a pearly cream colour, with straw-brown legs to match its rocky habitat.

Leucorchestris and *Carparachne,* the large desert spiders, are respectively known as White ladies and Wheeling spiders. *Leucorchestris arenicola* is the real 'Dancing white lady', because of its coloration and strange, prancing behaviour when threatened. *Carparachne* is known as the 'Golden wheeling spider'. Very pale off-white, these two genera are very similar in looks to *Palystes,* except for their colour and legs, which are armed with spines.

Pseudomicrommata is a monotypic genus. It is a smaller member of the family and lives in grasslands. Apart from its size, it is distinguished from the other members of the family by having well-defined red or reddish-brown bands down the body.

The sparassids are nocturnal in the wild, coming out at night to hunt. In built-up areas they may be active during the day owing to

J Visser

Palystella sexmaculatus *from central Namibia.*

N Larsen

New genus of Dune huntsman spider from the Kalahari Desert.

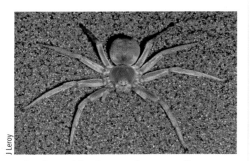

J Leroy

Wheeling spider, Carparachne aureoflava.

the comings and goings of humans. *Palystes* is most often seen indoors on walls, attracted by the insects that follow the light. Resting with its long legs outstretched, it will move away with great speed if it is disturbed. Its behaviour has given rise to a number of common names, such as Rain spider (as it often comes indoors before the rain, when insects are prevalent), Wall spider (because of its ambushing position on the wall) and Lizard-eating spider (as it is known to occasionally feed on the small Cape dwarf gecko, *Lygodactylus capensis*, and the marbled leaf-toed gecko, *Afrogecko porphyreus*).

The females of *Palystes castaneus* and *P. superciliosus* make a large bag of papery white silk and leaves. These bags of leaves are found in hedges or shrubs and in low base vegetation, and are attached to surrounding branches and leaves by strong strands of silk. The female crouches behind or below the nest, protecting her brood.

Eusparassus makes a retreat of papery white silk under rocks. This oval nest is firmly attached to the substrate and is difficult to move. Its entrance may be covered with bits of leaves. If the nest is pulled open when a collector lifts the rock above it, the spider darts out and runs around to the opposite side of the rock. (This behaviour often leads to the demise of the spider, as the collector may drop the rock in fright, crushing the spider.)

Leucorchestris is found only in the dune areas of the Namib Desert. It makes its burrow – a deep narrow tube into which the spider just manages to squeeze – on the flat desert surface. *Carparachne* digs a sloping burrow into the slip-face of the dune, lining it with blobs of sand and sticky webbing. When threatened, *Carparachne*, the smaller of the two, folds in its legs and throws itself down the side of the dune, cartwheeling at great speed. On reaching the bottom it rapidly burrows into the sand and disappears from view.

Pseudomicrommata makes a large nest in *Eragrostis* grass, and is confined to areas where this grass is found. *Palystella* is found in the dry areas of the Northern Cape, the Kalahari and Namibia, while the smaller *Panaretella* occurs in coastal forests.

Wall crab spiders

FAMILY: Selenopidae

GENERA: *Anyphops, Selenops*

> LIFESTYLE: Free-running, rock living
> HABITAT: In built-up areas; on or
> under bark; on rocks or in crevices
> of rocks
> SIZE: Medium to large, 6–23 mm
> ACTIVITY: Nocturnal
> DANGER: Harmless
> COLLECTING METHODS: Hand-to-jar;
> rock turning

Eye pattern of Selenops.

Eye pattern of Anyphops.

Wall crab spiders (also known as Flatties) are common in houses, especially in the eastern regions of southern Africa. Their distinguishing features are a flattened body, and legs that spread out in a crab-like fashion. Long spines are present at intervals on the thin legs. They usually sit face down on the wall. They are distinguished from Huntsman spiders (see p. 88) by the flattened body and the distinctive eyes. Six eyes form an anterior row; the posterior row consists of two larger eyes. In *Anyphops* the anterior row of eyes is recurved, while in *Selenops* they are fairly straight.

Selenopidae are large, mottled brown to black spiders, and are extremely agile and fast if they are disturbed.

These spiders are possibly most often seen indoors because their cryptic coloration makes them almost invisible on trees and rocks. Furthermore, their frozen stance

Wall crab spider, Selenops *sp.*

Anyphops *species with egg sac.*

makes for perfect camouflage when resting on anything but a plain-coloured wall. When moving undisturbed, their gait is similar to that of a large sparassid (see p. 88). With their flat bodies, they can disappear behind skirting boards and hanging pictures and into seemingly inaccessible places.

Eggs are laid in a disc-shaped, papery, smooth white cocoon, which is secured to the substrate. The discs, 5 cm in diameter, are seen against the sides of wooden beams and gumpoles supporting thatched roofs, in garden sheds and in outbuildings.

Wolf spider with egg case attached to spinnerets.

Wolf spiders

FAMILY: Lycosidae

GENERA: 31 including *Evippomma*, *Hippasa* (Funnel-web wolf spiders), *Lycosa* (Burrowing wolf spiders), *Geolycosa* (Burrowing wolf spiders), *Pardosa* (Sand wolf spiders), *Zenonina*, *Proevippa*, *Trabea*, *Tricassa*.
Pardosa is a smaller member of the family; they are creamy brown to black. Often the legs of the lycosids have a typically banded appearance.

> LIFESTYLE: Free-running, ground-living
> HABITAT: In built-up areas; in webbing, scrapes or free-running, under stones; on or under sand; on open ground; on rocks or in crevices of rocks; in and under leaf litter and rotting logs; near fresh water; on water; in semi-arid desert
> SIZE: Small to large, 3–30 mm
> ACTIVITY: Diurnal/Nocturnal
> DANGER: Harmless
> COLLECTING METHODS: Hand-to-jar; night collecting; pitfall trap; digging; rock turning

Wolf spider with spiderlings on abdomen.

'Lykos' is the Greek word for wolf, and just like their namesakes, these spiders are vagabonds that lie in wait to run down their prey. They are easily recognized by their characteristic eye pattern. The eyes are arranged in three rows. The anterior four eyes are very small and either straight or slightly procurved; the two larger posterior medians are situated on the vertical front of the carapace; and the two smaller posterior lateral eyes are above and to the sides of the head, making up the third row.

Most southern African species are pale creamy-brown to dark grey, with darker markings on the carapace and abdomen. The abdomen is oval and has brown, orange, grey and black chevron patterns. Often the legs of the lycosids have a typically banded appearance. Although they appear drab at first glance, on closer examination some species are quite beautiful.

Some species, which are pale cream in colour, present bold and attractive chevron markings and their chelicerae show a postbox red when they are threatened. The ventral aspect of the abdomen is sometimes jet black, with distinctive white markings.

Hippasa is a fairly large, olive-brown to black spider, with two rows of white spots on the abdomen and long, superior spinnerets rather like those of the Grass funnel-web spiders (see p. 60).

Pardosa and *Evippa* are the smaller members of the family and are creamy brown to black. *Zenonina* can be recognized by its triangular abdomen and its sandy habitat.

The habit of the female of carrying the egg sac attached to her spinnerets makes it possible to recognize the family even from a distance.

Free-roaming hunters, Wolf spiders are active both day and night, in and out of doors. They can be collected with ease at night, as their eyes reflect bright green under torchlight and they remain motionless as you approach. The smaller Wolf spiders – mainly *Pardosa*, which grows to 10 mm – roam freely among stones and low vegetation and are often seen on lawns. Some *Lycosa* species are also seen on lawns, especially if the grass is freshly mown. Some species of *Pardosa* are semi-aquatic and live near or on the water. *Evippa* have similar habits to *Pardosa*, but prefer desert and semi-arid regions.

The larger representatives, mainly *Lycosa*, appear to be quite dozy, but if disturbed will run away at speed, in leaps and jumps; or rear up, front legs raised in defence. *Geolycosa* and certain *Lycosa* species live in burrows similar to those of Trapdoor spiders, but without a trapdoor (see p. 113). It is possible that when revised, the *Geolycosa* species will have to be placed in a new genus, as it appears to be a northern hemisphere genus.

Hippasa is the exception to the rule in this family: it is sedentary, with behaviour similar to that of the agelenids (see p. 60). It builds a typical funnel-shaped web with a platform, like those of the agelenids. (An 'agelenid' in a funnel-web with an egg sac

N Larsen

Face of a Zimbabwean lycosid.

attached to the spinnerets must therefore be a lycosid, genus *Hippasa*.) *Tricassa* occurs on sandy beaches on the west coast of southern Africa. *Trabea* is found in open grassland habitats and under stones, while *Proevippa* ranges from grassland to the mountains of the eastern escarpment.

After laying and securing her eggs in a sac, the female lycosid attaches this 'ball' to her spinnerets, and it remains there until the young emerge. Often she can be seen traversing rough and stony terrain, with the egg sac seemingly being battered and bruised. However, this rough treatment does not appear to harm the eggs. When the spiderlings emerge from the egg sac after having completed their first moult, they climb onto their mother's abdomen and are carried about for several days. Should they fall off, they simply walk up a leg and back onto the abdomen again, or are lost forever, as the mother will not knowingly come back to look for them.

Dwarf hunting spiders and Dwarf armoured spiders

FAMILY: Oonopidae

DANGER: Harmless
COLLECTING METHODS: Sweep-netting; beating; hand-to-jar; pitfall trap; tullgren funnel; sifting; pooter; rock turning

Oonopidae is a family of small spiders (generally less than 3 mm in length) with six eyes, except for those living in termite nests, which are blind. They are divided into two distinct subfamilies: those with soft abdomens (Oonopinae) and those with abdomens covered with a hard shield or scutum (Gamasomorphinae). Oonopids are fairly common throughout southern Africa.

DWARF HUNTING SPIDERS

SUBFAMILY: Oonopinae

GENERA: *Oonops, Orchestina, Calculus, Australoonops, Sulsula, Telchius*

LIFESTYLE: Free-running, ground-living
HABITAT: In and under leaf litter and rotting logs; on bushes and plants or in low base vegetation; on or under grass
SIZE: Very small to small, 2–4 mm
ACTIVITY: Nocturnal

Eye pattern of **Orchestina**.

The abdomen of this subfamily is soft and clothed in fine, pale hairs. In general, it is paler in colour than Gamasomorphinae.

Oonopinae make no webs and are ground-living, hunting spiders. They run over the surface, often moving in a series of jerks. They are usually found under stones, leaf litter or dry vegetation. *Oonops* is sometimes found in bird nests. They are nocturnal, hiding in small retreats during the day.

DWARF ARMOURED SPIDERS

SUBFAMILY: Gamasomorphinae

GENERA: *Gamasomorpha, Opopaea, Nephrochirus, Dysderina, Pseudoscaphiella*

LIFESTYLE: Free-running, ground-living
HABITAT: In webbing, scrapes or free-running, under stones; in and under

leaf litter and rotting logs; in
semi-arid desert
SIZE: Tiny to small, 1–4 mm
ACTIVITY: Nocturnal

These are small, armoured oonopids with
two chitinous scutes covering the dorsal and
ventral sides of the abdomen. Most species
have six eyes. Some species, which live in
termite nests, are blind. The eyes are all light
in colour and are arranged in a compact
group. The carapace, scutes and legs are
orange-yellow to yellow, and the abdomen
is characteristically long and oval. Their
behaviour is similar to that of the Oonopinae.

Lateral view of a Dwarf armoured spider.

Six-eyed ground spiders

FAMILY: Orsolobidae

GENERA: *Afrilobus, Azanialobus*

LIFESTYLE: Free-running, ground-living
HABITAT: In and under leaf litter and
rotting logs; in forests
SIZE: Small, 3–5 mm
ACTIVITY: Diurnal/Nocturnal
DANGER: Harmless
COLLECTING METHODS: Hand-to-jar;
pitfall trap; tullgren funnel; pooter;
rock turning

Orsolobidae is a family of six-eyed, two-
clawed spiders. They are identified by the
presence of elevated tarsal organs that are

synapomorphic for the family. *Afrilobus* can
be distinguished from *Azanialobus* by its
abdominal markings. *Afrilobus* has a purplish
hue on the dorsal side, marked with pale
chevrons, while the abdomen of *Azanialobus*
is pale and uniform. *Afrilobus* has spines on
all eight legs; *Azanialobus* has spines only on
the first and second pairs of legs.

Collection of specimens from montane
forests in Malawi and KwaZulu-Natal suggests
a free-running, hunting existence in the leaf
litter and humus of the forest floor. However,
some species have been collected in the non-
forest biome of the Cederberg in the Western
Cape, where they roam freely among the low
scrub bushes.

Palp-footed spiders

FAMILY: Palpimanidae

GENERA: *Palpimanus, Diaphorocellus*

LIFESTYLE: Free-running, ground-living
HABITAT: In webbing, scrapes or free-
running, under stones; under bark;
on open ground; in desert to forests
SIZE: Small to medium-large, 3–11 mm
ACTIVITY: Nocturnal
DANGER: Harmless
COLLECTING METHODS: Hand-to-jar;
pitfall trap; rock turning

The carapace of Palpimanidae is sclerotized
and sub-oval in outline, with the head evenly
rounded and sloping back to the thoracic
region. The carapace and legs are orange,
red or maroon in colour. Characteristic of the
family are the greatly enlarged and armoured
front legs, especially the femora. The abdomen
is ovoid, with the cuticle leathery and the
epigastric region sclerotized, forming a scute
which encircles the pedicel. *Diaphorocellus*
usually has a purplish abdomen with light

Palpimanids rest with front legs drawn back.

Front legs of palpimanid showing scopulae.

spots on the dorsal aspect. The eye pattern of *Palpimanus* shows the posterior median eyes round and widely separated, while in *Diaphorocellus* the two posterior median eyes are triangular and subcontiguous.

Palp-footed spiders are found throughout southern Africa. They are slow-moving hunters that may be seen holding their enlarged front legs aloft. They make a small, irregular retreat web under a stone or under tree bark. Palpimanids prey on other spiders including *Carparachne* (Sparassidae), *Stegodyphus* (Eresidae), *Malaika* (Phyxelididae) and *Amaurobioides* (Anyphaenidae).

Nursery-web and Fishing spiders

FAMILY: Pisauridae

> SIZE: Medium to large, 8–30 mm (leg span may reach 60 mm)
> DANGER: Harmless
> COLLECTING METHODS: Beating; hand-to-jar; pitfall trap

NURSERY-WEB SPIDERS

SUBFAMILY: Pisaurinae

GENERA: 12 including *Euprosthenops, Euprosthenopsis, Chiasmopes, Cispius, Rothus, Tetragonophthalma*

> LIFESTYLE: Sedentary, web-bound; free-running, ground-living; free-running, plant-living
> HABITAT: In and up trees; on open ground; on bushes and plants or in low base vegetation; on or under grass
> ACTIVITY: Diurnal/Nocturnal

Nursery-web spiders may be recognized by their slender body and long legs with numerous spines. The elongated abdomen shows symmetrical patterns of black on a rufous to grey background. Some species have white bands running down the sides of the carapace and abdomen, but these markings are more characteristic of the subfamily *Thalassinae*.

The long legs are armed with numerous spines. At rest in the web, the spider most often holds the first two pairs of legs forward and close together. The legs have three claws on each tarsus. A colulus is present. The smaller *Euprosthenopsis* is a dark brown spider with pale lateral stripes running the length of the body. Both *Euprosthenops* and *Euprosthenopsis* have the anterior lateral eyes situated below lateral projections.

Euprosthenops is the largest member of this subfamily. It is a large, impressive-looking spider that builds its nursery web in the middle of woody shrubs, in trees (often *Acacia*) and in succulent plants. The web is a tent-like structure made of tough strands of silk. It slopes downwards at an oblique angle, often narrowing into a tunnel or into the base of the plant in which it is made. The spider hangs inverted within the fine, tent-like webbing, and if disturbed disappears with incredible speed into the retreat. This behaviour makes it one of the most difficult spiders to catch. Similarly, *Euprosthenopsis* and *Tetragonophthalma* are found on smaller sheet webs, situated among grass or low vegetation, with a retreat to one side entering a burrow. They also use speed to capture prey.

Chiasmopes has a pale median stripe dorsally and is delicate and slender, as is its web, which is generally made closer to the ground, in coarse grass or small bushes. When touched, the silk of its web breaks easily. *Chiasmopes* does not have eyes below the lateral projections on the carapace.

Cispius and *Rothus* are active, running hunters that pursue their prey in leaps and bounds across the substrate.

Females of the family make a spherical egg sac, which they carry in the chelicerae. The bulk of the egg sac hangs below the sternum, forcing the female to assume a tip-toed stance as she walks to keep the eggs safely above the substrate. The egg sac, like that of Wolf spiders (see p. 92), is

Funnel-web pisaurid, Euprosthenops *sp.*

Sheet-web pisaurid, Euprosthenopsis pulchella.

Crowned nursery-web spider, Rothus vittatus.

formed as a single ball that encloses the eggs. Just before the young emerge, the female attaches the egg sac to some leaves or twigs in low vegetation. She weaves a tent-like structure around it and, around this, a secondary framework of fine silk; hence the common name, Nursery-web spider. When the spiderlings emerge they are 'trapped' within this nursery, and remain there for one or two instars before biting their way out. The female remains in the nursery throughout this time to guard her young.

FISHING SPIDERS

SUBFAMILY: Thalassinae

GENERA: *Thalassius, Dolomedes*

LIFESTYLE: Free-running, ground-living
HABITAT: Near fresh water; on water
ACTIVITY: Diurnal

Thalassinae are impressive-looking spiders, with bright white borders to the body prominent in some species. The dorsal aspect of the abdomen often shows numerous colour patterns within a chocolate-brown background.

Thalassius spinosissimus *with speckled pattern.*

Unmarked Thalassius spinosissimus *with an* Amietia fuscigula *tadpole.*

Distinctively, the genera of this subfamily stand with their long legs spread out, equally spaced and encircling the whole body.

Thalassius lives and hunts near pools of water with side vegetation. It moves rapidly on both land and water, and can often be seen drifting on the surface of the water, being moved along by the breeze. Some of the larger species catch tadpoles and even small fish. *Dolomedes* is similar to *Thalassius* but is more common in the northern hemisphere.

Like the other pisaurids, the female carries the egg sac with her until the spiderlings are about to emerge. She guards the spiderlings until they are ready to leave the nursery.

Jumping spiders

FAMILY: Salticidae

GENERA: 63 including *Cyrba, Cosmophasis, Euophrys, Habrocestum, Hasarius, Heliophanus, Hyllus, Marengo, Myrmarachne, Natta, Pachyballus, Phlegra, Portia, Thyene, Menemerus*

LIFESTYLE: Free-running, ground-living; free-running, plant-living
HABITAT: Found in almost every environment
SIZE: Small to large, 3–17 mm
ACTIVITY: Diurnal
DANGER: Harmless
COLLECTING METHODS: Sweep-netting; beating; hand-to-jar; pitfall trap; sifting; rock turning; tree trap

These spiders have the best vision of all the hunting spiders, and if you get close enough you will notice the intensity of their stare. Light reflecting from the back of the eyes makes it appear as if the spider is actually following your movements, and this gives it an anthropomorphic quality.

Most of the genera are between 5 and 10 mm in length. You will need a magnifying glass to see not only the attentive look but, in the case of many of the males, also the pedipalps adorned with iridescent hairs and their colourful bodies (the common name for the male of the genus *Portia* is the Dandy).

In most species, the cephalothorax is squarish in shape and larger than the abdomen. The eye pattern is diagnostic: a pair of large anterior median eyes in the centre front of the carapace, with the anterior lateral eyes raised and to the side. The posterior eyes are set above and to the sides of the head. (Salticids are free-roaming hunters that 'jump' on their prey. For this they require the stereoscopic vision that the large median eyes make possible.)

N Larsen

Thyene inflata *with blowfly (Calliphoridae).*

N Larsen

Menemerus bifurcus, a common Jumping spider.

N Larsen

Face showing enlarged posterior median eyes.

Jumping spiders are active, diurnal hunters, moving around with quick darts and long leaps. Before each leap, the spider connects an anchor line to the substrate with an attachment disc; if the spider misses its landing or does not land on solid ground, it can haul itself back to safety (this is the original bungee jump!). The smaller eyes around the large anterior median eyes perceive movement. Once the prey has been located, the spider will rapidly turn and align itself with the target, looking directly at it. The movable retinas of the main eyes compensate for the spider's overall narrow vision, and it is the reflection of this movement that gives the eyes their gaze-like quality. (The good eyesight of Jumping spiders can be demonstrated by setting up a mirror in front of a male. The spider reacts to the mirror image as if it is a real conspecific opponent.)

Some species of Salticidae spiders mimic ants, with which they sometimes live. Holding their first pair of legs aloft to mimic feelers, they take on the coloration and appearance of the ants and may even mimic the ants' typical searching gait. Other spiders also mimic ants, but none as well as the Jumping spiders.

Salticidae do not spin a web, but make a sac-like nest from thick white silk attached to vegetation. It is used as a retreat or as an incubator for the egg sac. These nests are found on the florescence of grass tufts, in rolled-up leaves or flowers, in cavities under rocks, and sometimes even in the empty shells of dried-out beetles. Salticidae may also use the bulbous and enlarged thorns of some *Acacia* species as a retreat. If you can find the small hole or holes at the confluence of these thorns and split them open, you will probably find the web retreat, and in many cases the spider as well. Salticids can often be found in old vacated *Palystes* egg sacs.

Spitting spiders

FAMILY: Scytodidae

GENUS: *Scytodes*

> **LIFESTYLE: Free-running, ground living**
> **HABITAT: In built-up areas; on rocks or in crevices of rocks; in and under leaf litter and rotting logs**
> **SIZE: Small to medium-large, 3.5–15 mm (leg span up to 33 mm); female larger than male**
> **ACTIVITY: Nocturnal**
> **DANGER: Harmless**
> **COLLECTING METHODS: Hand-to-jar; pitfall trap; pooter; rock turning**

Scytodes testudo *with egg sac.*

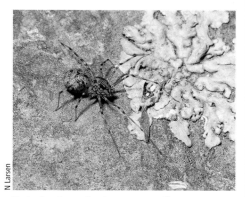

Scytodes thoracica *is a cosmopolitan Spitting spider.*

Scytodes is easily recognized by the shape of its carapace, which is lofty and rounded in the thoracic region, sloping downwards towards the head. It has six eyes arranged in three well-separated pairs. Its colour varies from pale yellow to dark brown, with dark, symmetrical patterns on its dorsal aspect. The banded legs are long and delicate.

Some species are found in and around human habitations, especially in dark corners near rubble and dustbins. They move slowly, stalking their prey, and are often found in closets and dark cupboards.

Spitting spiders are hunters. When prey is located, it is immobilized by the fine strings of a venomous, sticky silk secretion that the spider ejects from its fangs. By rapidly

vibrating the chelicerae from side to side, *Scytodes* is able to zigzag the sticky strings across and over the prey to form a net, fixing the prey to the substrate. Some South African species eject their sticky venom longitudinally and not in a zigzag pattern, as the European species do.

The egg sac is carried in the chelicerae, rather in the same manner as the pholcids (see p. 67). Preying on fishmoths and other soft-bodied pests, these are definitely spiders to be encouraged in the home.

Violin spiders and Six-eyed sand spiders

FAMILY: Sicariidae

Violin spiders
GENUS: *Loxosceles*

> **LIFESTYLE: Free-running, ground-living**
> **HABITAT: In built-up areas; on or under bark; in webbing, scrapes or free-running, under stones; in and under leaf litter and rotting logs; in forests; in disused holes; in caves**
> **SIZE: Medium to medium-large, 8–15 mm (leg span up to 40 mm); female slightly larger than male**
> **ACTIVITY: Nocturnal**
> **DANGER: Venomous**
> **COLLECTING METHODS: Hand-to-jar; night collecting; pitfall trap; sifting**

Violin spiders are often mistaken for members of the family Pholcidae (see p. 67). They have six eyes arranged in three well-separated pairs. Their colour varies from grey to rich red-brown, with darker markings on the abdomen. They have a characteristic dark brown to black violin-shaped marking on the carapace, which gives them their common name. The carapace is relatively flat, with the

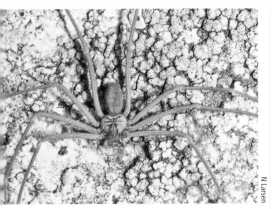

N Larsen

Violin spider showing violin markings on the carapace.

N Larsen

Violin spider, Loxosceles *sp.*

abdomen oval-shaped and the legs long and slender. A long, obvious colulus is present.

Loxosceles is never web-bound. It roams freely at night in search of prey; it is this behaviour that readily distinguishes it from the pholcids, which are web-bound. The natural

Eye pattern and marking of Loxosceles *carapace.*

habitat of the savanna species is under rocks and logs, beneath the bark of fallen trees, in old termite nests, among rubble and in deserted human habitations. Two species are cave dwellers. One of the cave-dwelling species, *L. parrami*, has been artificially introduced into human habitation on the Witwatersrand and is found in the cracks and crevices of walls, behind picture frames and in dark corners of cupboards and drawers. This is not a commonly encountered genus.

The cytotoxic venom of *Loxosceles* can cause a nasty ulcerating wound, rarely involving severe secondary infection. The resulting tissue damage can leave a disfiguring scar which may require plastic surgery.

Six-eyed sand spiders
GENUS: *Sicarius*

LIFESTYLE: Free-running, ground-living
HABITAT: On or under sand: in semi-arid desert
SIZE: Medium to medium-large.
8–15 mm (leg span up to 30 mm)
ACTIVITY: Diurnal/Nocturnal
DANGER: Venomous
COLLECTING METHOD: Hand-to-jar

Sicarius is a six-eyed spider with a flattened body, similar to the selenopids (see p. 91), and a leathery integument, which is usually covered with sand particles. The legs are extended sideways and held close to the substrate. The eyes are in three pairs and set on the front of the flattened carapace, giving the spider a squint-eyed appearance.

Sicarius lives on and in the sand in the arid to semi-arid western regions of southern Africa. Its brownish body, often covered with sand particles, blends in well with the environment, and when stationary it is almost impossible to see. A sudden dash and dive

Six-eyed sand spider, Sicarius testaceus.

Sicarius testaceus *with sand particles trapped between setae on the body.*

into the sand invariably gives it away; it is amazing how quickly it can disappear by throwing sand over its body with its legs.

The spider makes no web of any kind and is a hunter, relying on ambush to overcome its prey. Equipped with a stridulatory organ, it is said to produce a faint humming sound. In captivity, *Sicarius* has been known to live for several years.

Sicarius is normally found in unpopulated, arid areas and is reluctant to bite. A recent case, where the spider was positively identified, did not result in any serious injury. The reviser, when catching desert reptiles that would dive into the

sand, often picked up these spiders by hand without ever receiving a bite.

Sicarius has a virulent cytotoxic venom, but its effect on humans is not well documented. From experimental bites on rabbits, the venom destroys not only the tissue structure in the vicinity of the bite but also tissue throughout the body, causing massive internal haemorrhaging and necrosis.

Long-spinnered spiders

FAMILY: Hersiliidae

GENERA: *Hersilia* (Long-spinnered bark spiders), *Hersiliola* (Long-spinnered rock spiders), *Tyrotama* (Long-spinnered stone nest spiders)

LIFESTYLE: Free-running, ground living; free-running, plant living
HABITAT: On or under bark; in webbing, scrapes or free-running, under stones; on rocks or in crevices of rocks
SIZE: Small to medium, 5–10 mm
ACTIVITY: Diurnal
DANGER: Harmless
COLLECTING METHODS: Hand-to-jar; rock turning

Hersiliids are flat spiders with two long spinnerets protruding far past the rear of the abdomen. They are usually seen resting upside-down with legs outstretched on the bark of trees or the sides of rocks. The eyes are generally in two strongly recurved rows, situated on a large protuberance at the front of the carapace. Their colour varies from grey to brown and even a speckled black; reportedly, they may undergo a certain amount of colour change to blend in with their background environment. The carapace and abdomen are flattened, and the

Long-spinnered bark spider, Hersilia *sp.*

Long-spinnered stone nest spider, Tyrotama arida.

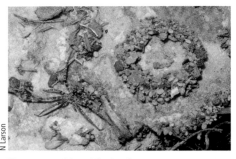

Tyrotama arida *with circular retreat.*

abdomen is most often wider behind than it is in front. The legs are fairly robust and are held out in a star-like fashion; they have the same cryptic coloration as the spider's body.

Hersilia is found on the bark of trees and is difficult to see. The flattened body casts almost no shadow and the speckled coloration blends in with the background. This camouflage is destroyed only when the spider moves when it is disturbed. It is reported that should you mark the eight

points at which the legs rest, then disturb the spider so it moves away, it will return after a time and take up the identical position.

Hersiliola and *Tyrotama* (formerly *Tama*) are found on and among rocks. Their behaviour is similar to that of *Hersilia*, but *Tyrotama* is said to spin an irregular web rather like that of the pholcids (see p. 67). These spiders also make a nest of loose webbing encompassing small stones and leaf debris. This retreat may appear as a spreading network of fine threads extending outwards for up to 23 cm. The spinnerets of *Tyrotama* are not always obvious, as the spider curls them up onto the posterior abdomen.

Hersiliids enswathe their prey by emitting silk from the spinnerets while rotating the spinnerets rapidly across and around the victim.

Burrowing spiders and Ant-eating spiders

FAMILY: Zodariidae

GENERA: 17 including *Capheris, Psammorygma* and *Cydrela* (Trapdoor zodariids), *Caesetius* (Sand swimmers), *Psammoduon* (Back-flip spiders), *Diores* (Ant-eating zodariids), *Chariobas* (Grass-stitchers)

LIFESTYLE: Free-running, ground-living; sedentary, burrow-living
HABITAT: In webbing, scrapes or free-running, under stones; on or under sand; on open ground; in burrows; in semi-arid desert; in association with insects
SIZE: Very small to large, 2–30 mm
ACTIVITY: Diurnal/Nocturnal
DANGER: Harmless
COLLECTING METHODS: Hand-to-jar; night collecting; pitfall trap; rock turning

Zodariids are eight-eyed hunting spiders that differ greatly in appearance. In some genera, the exoskeleton of the carapace and legs is thick and tough and looks like armour. The legs are usually equal in length and thickness. The anterior spinnerets of zodariids are usually the longest and are situated close together; their unique shape is a useful taxonomic tool. The posterior and median spinnerets are short (visible under moderate magnification). In most genera the body is large and robust, but *Diores* – mimicking the ants among which it lives – is small and more delicate.

Psammorygma, *Capheris* and *Cydrela* make tube-like burrows with lids, like those of the Trapdoor spiders (see p. 113). *Caesetius* is found under stones and is said to make a sac-like nest, which hangs down like a bag when the stone is lifted. Some *Caesetius* species are adapted to living in sand and, if threatened, can rapidly burrow head-first into the sand.

Diores is diurnal and can be seen running furiously back and forth with ants. It spins a bag-like retreat under rocks, on rocks near the ant colony or on the ant mound itself. The retreat is often camouflaged with pebbles and debris, and at night the spider takes refuge in this hideaway. Some authors compare the retreat to an igloo.

Chariobas has a slender, elongated body and is found on restios and other grasses.

Decorated burrowing zodariid, Psammorygma *sp.*

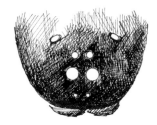

Zodariid eye pattern.

Zodariid spinnerets.

Back-flip spider, Psammoduon canosum.

These medium-sized spiders roll and stitch leaf edges together to form a retreat. A specimen of *Chariobas* was collected from the southern Cape, which extended the family's maximum size from 21 mm to 30 mm.

Psammoduon is very interesting in that it dives into soft dune sand. Although its common name is Back-flip spider, this spider does a forward roll into the sand, back downwards, and uses the spines on its legs to tunnel deeper into the sand. It is believed that *Psammoduon* preys on *Thysanura* (Silverfish).

Free-living arboreal spiders

Running spiders

FAMILY: Philodromidae

GENERA: *Philodromus, Thanatus, Hirriusa, Ebo, Tibellus, Suemus, Gephyrota*

> **LIFESTYLE: Free-running, sedentary; plant-living, ground-living**
> **HABITAT: In and up trees; on rocks or in crevices of rocks; on bushes and plants or in low base vegetation; on or under grass; in and under leaf litter and rotting logs; in houses**
> **SIZE: Small to large, 3–16 mm**
> **ACTIVITY: Diurnal/Nocturnal**
> **DANGER: Harmless**
> **COLLECTING METHODS: Sweep-netting; beating; hand-to-jar; tree trap**

The philodromids have a slightly flattened body with slender, laterigrade legs that are mostly of equal length and thickness. Claw tufts are present on the first two pairs of legs. There are teeth on the promargin of the chelicerae, unlike those of the thomisids (see p. 107). The eyes are almost the same size and are positioned in two recurved rows. Most species have an elongate to oval abdomen, often with chevron markings, which is flattened dorsoventrally. The mottled yellow and brown body blends with the spider's habitat. In *Ebo*, the second pair of legs is much longer than the other legs.

Most species are tree- or grass-living and are wanderers. As with other wanderers, they are swift and aggressive in pursuing prey. *Philodromus* is found on trunks of trees, on bushes and in houses. *Tibellus* is of slender build and more often collected while grass-sweeping. *Hirriusa* and

Grass running spider, Tibellus minor.

Plant running spider, Philodromus *species*.

Thanatus are cursorial. *Ebo* is most often found after beating *Acacia* trees.

This family was previously regarded as a subfamily of Thomisidae, but differ in that thomisids have the first two pairs of legs enlarged. Although much smaller, Philodromidae also bear a resemblance to the family Sparassidae (see p. 88).

Crab spiders

FAMILY: Thomisidae

The family Thomisidae consists of seven subfamilies – Thomisinae, Bominae, Stiphropodinae, Stephanopinae, Strophiinae, Dietinae and Coriarachninae – with 37 genera. We will consider only three subfamilies. There is little information on the remaining subfamilies, which are in the process of revision.

> **LIFESTYLE: Sedentary, ground-living; sedentary, plant-living**
> **HABITAT: In and up trees; on or under bark; in webbing, scrapes or free-running, under stones; on rocks or in crevices of rocks; on bushes and plants or in low base vegetation; on or under grass; on flowers and leaves**
> **SIZE: Very small to large, 2–23 mm**
> **ACTIVITY: Diurnal**
> **DANGER: Harmless**
> **COLLECTING METHODS: Sweep-netting; beating; hand-to-jar; rock turning**

Crab spiders are expert ambushers and do not spin webs. They patiently wait for prey to alight near them. They appear sluggish and lethargic, only to be transformed into a flash of movement as they pounce on and over prey that strays too near. They rely on touch rather than sight to capture their prey, and on their stillness and coloration to protect them from

predators. They are formidable spiders and will attack insects and other spiders much larger than themselves. They have a potent venom, which can kill a bee within seconds. Holding the prey in their chelicerae, they literally suck it dry, discarding the empty shell of the insect.

SUBFAMILY: Thomisinae

GENERA: 20, including *Thomisus, Ansiae* (Flower crab spiders), *Runcinia* (Grass crab spiders), *Synema* (African mask crab spiders), *Diaea, Tmarus* (Bark crab spiders), *Monaeses, Misumenops, Pherecydes* (Bark crab spiders), *Xysticus* (Ground crab spiders)

N Larsen

Flower crab spider, Thomisus australis, *with captured bee.*

Crab spider, Diaea *sp.*

New Bark crab spider species, Tmarus *sp.*

African mask crab spider, Synema imitator.

New African mask crab spider, Synema *sp.*

Stalk-eyed crab spider, Pherecydes tuberculatus.

Ground crab spider, Xysticus *sp.*

Eye pattern of Xysticus.

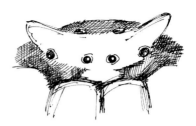

Eye pattern of Thomisus.

Eye pattern of Runcinia.

Eye pattern of Tmarus.

Crab spiders are well known and have been researched in detail in South Africa by Dr Ansie Dippenaar-Schoeman of the Plant Protection Research Institute. The superficial resemblance of some species to crabs, as well as their ability to move sideways and backwards with ease, have given them their common name.

Most species have a short, wide and slightly flattened body, with the legs directed sideways and with the two front pairs usually longer and more powerful than the other legs. The eye pattern varies between the genera, but it is distinctive of the family and highly diagnostic. The lateral eyes are either separate or on conjoined tubercles. In Thomisinae, the eyes of many genera are situated on distinct tubercles (as in *Thomisus*) or on a carina (as in *Runcinia*). In others, the eyes are on small swellings.

Thomisinae are usually found on plants. In general, they are sluggish spiders. *Thomisus* is common on flowers. It has the ability to slowly change colour depending on the shade of the flower, and vary in colour from white to yellow to pink. *Misumenops*, coloured in bright greens and reds, is also found on flowers.

Thomisids found on grass usually have long, narrow bodies. Their colour is that of the grass on which they are found, with dark longitudinal lines resembling the veins of the grass blades, as in *Monaeses* and *Runcinia*. Genera found on seeds are hairy and have a spiky appearance.

Tmarus is found on the bark of trees and *Pherecydes* in the bark crevices. *Xysticus*, a drab, dark brown spider in subfamily Coriarachninae, is found on and under stones and sometimes on tree bark.

SUBFAMILY: Bominae

GENERA: *Holopelus, Avelis, Parabomis, Felsina, Thomisops*

Bominae are small spiders, characterized by a globose body, a thick, granular integument and short legs. They live on plants, mainly grasses and flowering herbs.

SUBFAMILY: Dietinae

GENERA: *Hewittia, Oxytate* (Green grass crab spiders), *Paramystaria, Sylligma, Zametopias*

There is very little information available on these genera, except for *Oxytate*. *Oxytate* is a green, slender-bodied spider that sits concealed on blades of grass and appears to be fairly common.

Lynx spiders

Family: Oxyopidae

GENERA: *Oxyopes* (Golden lynx spiders), *Peucetia* (Green lynx spiders), *Hamataliwa* (Dome-head lynx spiders)

> LIFESTYLE: Free-running, plant-living
> HABITAT: On bushes and plants or in low base vegetation; on or under grass; on flowers or leaves
> SIZE: Small to large, 5–23 mm (some larger species of *Peucetia* may have a leg span of up to 40 mm)
> ACTIVITY: Diurnal
> DANGER: Harmless
> COLLECTING METHODS: Sweep-netting; beating; hand-to-jar

Lynx spiders may be immediately recognized by the numerous spines standing out at right angles on their legs, and in some species, by their bright colours. They have a high and angular carapace that is flattened in front, with a wide clypeus and a distinctive eye pattern. The abdomen tapers to a point at the rear.

Oxyopes and *Hamataliwa* are smaller than *Peucetia*, which can display a variety of colours, from bright green to yellow and maroon markings. *Oxyopes*, which is very

Green grass crab spider, Oxytate argenteooculata.

common on plants, also varies in colour from bright yellow-green to dull brown or grey. *Hamataliwa* is a rather drab brown colour, but is easily recognized as a member of the family by its typical spines. Its most obvious

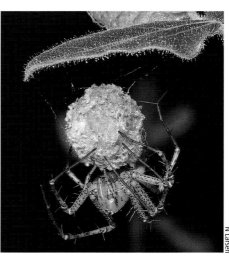

Green lynx spider, Peucetia nicolae, *with egg sac.*

N Larsen

Lynx spider, Peucetia striata, *guarding spiderlings.*

identifying feature is the presence of little tufts of hair growing out above the eyes. The carapace is dome-shaped.

Lynx spiders live on plants. Their common name is indicative of their cat-like behaviour of stalking and pouncing on prey. They can be seen leaping with great ease through the leaves of low shrubs and bushes, either chasing prey or escaping from predators. Some species can jump more than 2 cm into the air to seize a passing insect in full light.

Some species of *Peucetia* are more sedentary, favouring glandular plants. Insects become trapped on these plants, thus providing instant food for the Lynx spider inhabitant.

Oxyopidae do not make webs. Silk is used as a safety line when the spider is jumping, and for anchoring the egg sac to vegetation. The female fastens the egg sac to a twig or suspends it among silken threads between twigs and leaves, and guards the eggs until they hatch. During this time, she does not eat, and she dies when the eggs hatch.

N Larsen

Golden lynx spider, Oxyopes jacksoni.

MYGALOMORPHS

Mygalomorphs belong to the infraorder Mygalomorphae, which is thought to be a primitive group. They are characterized by having two pairs of book lungs and paraxial chelicerae that strike forwards and downwards. Most mygalomorphs are medium to very large spiders and many of them are sedentary ground-dwellers.

African purse-web spiders

FAMILY: Atypidae

GENUS: *Calommata* (African purse-web spiders)

> **LIFESTYLE: Sedentary, ground-living**
> **HABITAT: Silken tube**
> **SIZE: Medium to medium-large, 9–11 mm**
> **ACTIVITY: Diurnal/Nocturnal**
> **DANGER: Harmless**
> **COLLECTING METHOD: Hand-to-jar**

The atypids are a small family of spiders that live permanently in a silken tube. Their large chelicerae are dorsally expanded with long fangs and enormously elongated endites. Their eyes are situated on a transverse protuberance near the centre of the cephalic area. The size of their legs, especially the first pair, is greatly reduced.

A single species, *Calommata simoni*, is known from southern Africa. The female is about 9–11 mm long; it spends its entire life within a silken tube sealed at both ends and camouflaged with bits of debris. A small portion of the tube protrudes above the ground; a burrow extends for about 30 cm into the ground.

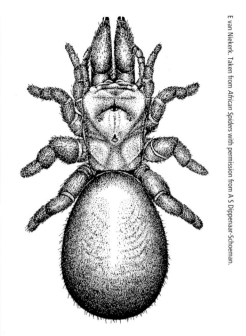

Calommata simoni *female.*

The section above the ground resembles a narrow purse, hence the common name. The spider attacks any insect that lands on the tube by biting through the tube and impaling the victim with its long fangs. After injecting the venom and immobilizing its prey, the spider pulls it through a hole in the tube (cut by the chelicerae for this purpose), consumes the prey and ejects the remains through the same hole. The spider then sets about repairing the damaged tube and awaits its next victim.

Calommata may be very aggressive if taken from its tube-web home.

Calommata simoni has not been collected in South Africa since the 1920s. However, males have recently been collected from the Pretoria area, the Free State and Zimbabwe. From the male genitalia it appears that more than one species occurs in the region.

Trapdoor baboon spiders

FAMILY: Barychelidae

GENERA: *Pisenor, Sipalolasma*

> LIFESTYLE: Sedentary, ground-living
> HABITAT: In webbing or scrapes,
> under stones; in burrows
> SIZE: Medium-large to very large,
> 12–32 mm
> ACTIVITY: Nocturnal
> DANGER: Harmless
> COLLECTING METHODS: Hand-to-jar;
> pitfall trap; digging; rock turning

Trapdoor baboon spiders are much smaller than the Theraphosidae (see p. 119). They also differ in that the apical segment of the posterior lateral spinnerets is shorter than the rest, and the anterior lobe of the maxillae is only weakly developed. The barychelids have two claws, with the scopulae on the tarsi of the first two pairs of legs well developed and iridescent. The carapace and legs are uniformly covered in setae. The carapace is as high in front of the fovea as it is behind.

In *Pisenor* the clypeus is absent and the anterior eyes are widely spaced. In *Sipalolasma* a clypeus is present and the eight eyes are grouped slightly further back on the carapace. The fovea is a deep, circular pit. Male *Sipalolasma* spiders have a tibial spur.

Most species build a silk-lined burrow in the ground. The burrow often has a 'Y' shape, either with both entrances open or with one

Trapdoor baboon spider.

ending blind just below the surface. When digging up the burrow, you may find the spider hiding in the closed-off tunnel. Trapdoor baboon spiders are aggressive and can move swiftly if threatened.

Cork-lid trapdoor spiders

FAMILY: Ctenizidae

GENUS: *Stasimopus*

> LIFESTYLE: Sedentary, ground-living
> HABITAT: In burrows
> SIZE: Large to very large, 22–42 mm
> ACTIVITY: Nocturnal
> DANGER: Harmless
> COLLECTING METHODS: Hand-to-jar;
> digging; pitfall trap

The Ctenizidae are large spiders. The female has bands of short, stout, thorn-like spines on the lateral surface of the third and fourth pairs of legs. Most of the species have a short, thick-set body lacking the hairy appearance of the family Theraphosidae (see p. 119). They are equipped with a rastellum, a spiny rake on the outer portion of the chelicerae, which they use to dig tubular burrows. The shortish legs are covered with spines and are usually robust.

All species dig burrows, which vary in shape and design but all of which are protected by a hinged, tight-fitting, reinforced lid. The burrow is almost invisible when the lid is closed. When threatened by predators, the spider uses the spines on its short, robust legs to grip the burrow wall and bottom of the trapdoor. It displays amazing strength in holding the trapdoor shut.

Not much has been written about the behaviour of Trapdoor spiders because their secluded lifestyle makes them difficult to study.

This family is distributed in the northern and eastern regions of southern Africa.

Cork-lid trapdoor spider, Stasimopus *species.*

Wafer-lid trapdoor spiders

FAMILY: Cyrtaucheniidae

> **LIFESTYLE: Sedentary, ground-living**
> **HABITAT: In burrows; in semi-arid desert**
> **SIZE: Medium to medium-large, 8–15 mm**
> **ACTIVITY: Nocturnal**
> **DANGER: Harmless**
> **COLLECTING METHODS: Hand-to-jar; digging**

Wafer-lid trapdoor spider, Homostola *species.*

SUBFAMILY: Cyrtaucheniinae

GENUS: *Homostola*

Carapace of Homostola.

SUBFAMILY: Aporoptychinae

GENUS: *Ancylotrypa*

Wafer-lid trapdoor spiders have a rastellum present in both South African genera. *Homostola*, known only from female specimens, has a slightly hairy carapace with a strongly arched head. The fovea is broad and procurved, and the eyes are set on a

Horned baboon spider, Ceratogyrus brachycephalus.

Theraphosid spiders are found throughout southern Africa, generally in the warmer, more arid areas. They live underground, in open-ended, silk-lined burrows, emerging only at night to hunt and never moving very far from the burrow. (Males may, however, be found wandering freely in search of a mate.)

Normally slow-moving, Baboon spiders can be taunted into aggressive action. When provoked, they will rear up, forelegs in the air, exposing the blood-red scopulae on the promargins of the endites and chelicerae, and black underparts.

Recent observations have suggested that the burrow entrances of the different genera vary. It has been found, for example, that those of *Ceratogyrus* are flush with the surrounding substrate while those of *Pterinochilus* and *Augacephalus* are raised some 2 cm above the substrate, with grass, leaves or twigs woven into the extended silk lining.

Much in demand as pets, Baboon spiders have been known to live as long as 20 to 25 years in captivity. Once removed from a mature burrow, they are unable to dig a new one as they do not have a rastellum on the chelicerae. In captivity, they construct a sheet-like mass of web on the substrate, attached to high points, giving a hammock-like appearance. They may then take up a position in the corner of the sheet or below one of the raised points.

Owing to their size (and especially the size of the chelicerae), Baboon spiders can inflict an extremely painful bite. The neurotoxic venom is only mildly toxic to man. That of the Lesser baboon spider, *Harpactirella lightfooti*, from the southwestern Cape, is said to be dangerous to man. This is incorrect, however, as its bite does not appear to be any more serious than those of the other genera, resulting in 1–18 hours of intense localized pain.

Golden starburst baboon spider, Augacephalus junodi.

Lightfoot's lesser baboon spider, Harpactirella lightfooti.

Lesser baboon spider, Harpactirella, *a new species.*

Glossary

Anal tubercle Tubercle at the end of the abdomen, bearing the anus.

Anterior Towards the front (see Posterior).

Anthropomorphic Having human characteristics (Anthropomorphism: The attribution of human form or behaviour to an animal).

Arachnid A class of arthropods characterized by having simple eyes and four pairs of legs.

Araneomorph spiders So-called 'true spiders', having diaxial fangs and tracheal spiracles.

Arboreal Living in or among trees or bushes (see Terrestrial).

Arthropoda A group of organisms, all of which possess an exoskeleton and jointed limbs.

Book lung A chamber connected with the atmosphere that the spider uses for breathing.

Calamistrum A row of curved, toothed setae on the metatarsus of the fourth leg of cribellate spiders, used to comb out silk from the cribellum.

Caput The 'head' section of the carapace.

Carapace The hard shield covering the top of the cephalothorax.

Caudal Concerning the tail.

Cephalothorax The fused head and thorax of a spider.

Chelicerae The first pair of appendages on the cephalothorax, used for biting, chewing and grasping; the fangs form the piercing part of these appendages.

Chevron A pattern consisting of one or more 'V'-shaped stripes, seen on the dorsal aspect of the abdomen of certain spiders.

Chitinous Covered with a nitrogen-containing polysaccharide, forming a material of great strength.

Clavate setae Club-shaped bristles.

Clypeus The area between the front row of eyes and the edge of the carapace.

Colulus A small protuberance, usually conical, representing the remnant of the cribellum.

Conspecific Belonging to the same species.

Contiguous Touching along the side or boundary; in contact.

Coxa First segment of legs and pedipalps.

Cribellate Having a cribellum (see Ecribellate).

Cribellum A flattened, sieve-like spinning plate, situated in front of the spinnerets of certain spiders containing thousands of tiny spigots.

Cryptozoic Inhabiting leaf litter and other hidden habitats.

Cryptic spiders The spiders that live in forest leaf litter or are camouflaged and thus not seen.

Cursorial Having limbs adapted for running.

Cytotoxic Venom which causes cell destruction

Diaxial The term applied to chelicerae when the fangs oppose each other.

Dimorphism Existing in two forms (used here to indicate the great size or form difference that exists between the male and female).

Diurnal Active during the day (see Nocturnal).

Dorsal The upper surface (see Ventral).

Ecdysis Another name for moulting, during which the old exoskeleton is shed and replaced by a new one.

Ecribellate Lacking a cribellum (see Cribellate).

Endite The modified coxa of the pedipalp (see Maxilla).

Entelegyne The term given to those spiders with complicated reproductive organs.

Epigastric furrow The ventral transverse opening, in both sexes, that is situated in line with the book lung openings.

Epigynum The sclerotized area around the opening of the female genitalia.

Exuviae The old skin once shed.

Fang The piercing part of the chelicerae, through which runs the venom duct.

Fovea A pit or depression near the centre of the carapace; corresponds to the attachment of muscles to the sucking stomach.

Genus A group, used in classifying organisms, consisting of a number of similar species (plural: genera).

Geotaxis Taxis in which the stimulus is gravitational force; thus, when a spider hangs upside-down under its web, it is said to be in negative geotaxis.

Glabrous Refers to integument without setae (see Hirsute).

Globose Globe-like in shape.

Haplogene The term given to those spiders with simple reproductive organs.